The Country Houses, Castles and Mansions of Berwickshire

Sir James Miller, of Manderston House, was Master of the Berwickshire Hunt from 1897 to 1906. It is believed to be the oldest Hunt in Scotland, dating from at least the early 1600s when the Earl of Home maintained a pack of hounds at his own expense, and the hunt was fully established by the middle of the following century. This 1904 photograph shows James Payne, the Manderston stud groom, with his immaculately-groomed four-in-hand ready to drive off for a meeting of the hunt. The stable block contained accommodation for the stud staff and the 1901 census shows Payne as living there with his wife Margaret and their three sons, along with six younger grooms for whom he had responsibility.

Stenlake Publishing Ltd

Text © Bernard Byrom, 2016
First Published in the United Kingdom, 2016
by Stenlake Publishing Limited
54–58 Mill Square, Catrine, KA5 6RD
www.stenlake.co.uk

ISBN 9781840337297

Printed by
Blissetts
Roslin Road
Acton
W3 8DH

The shallow stone-lined well in the grounds of Spottiswoode House.

Acknowledgements

Further reading

The books, newspapers and websites listed below were the principal ones used by the author during his research:

Robert Chambers, *The Picture of Scotland*, 1828
John Bartholomew, *Gazetteer of the British Isles*, 1887
James Denham, *Village Kirks of the Borders of Scotland*, 2013
F.H. Groome, *Ordnance Gazetteer of Scotland*, 1882–84
Elizabeth Layhe, *The History of Berwickshire's Towns and Villages*, 1894
C.A. Strang, *An Illustrated Architectural Guide to the Scottish Borders and Berwick*, 1994
George Tancred Weens, *The Annals of a Border Club*, 1899
Ordnance Gazetteer of Scotland, 1882–1885
The County Directory of Scotland (various years)
Berwickshire Advertiser
Dundee Courier

Glasgow Herald
Southern Reporter
Yorkshire Post & Leeds Intelligencer

British Listed Buildings website:
 www.britishlistedbuildings.co.uk
Historic Scotland website: www.historic-scotland.gov.uk
Undiscovered Scotland website:
www.undiscoveredscotland.co.uk
Dunse History Society website: dunsehistorysociety.co.uk
Stichill Village website: www.stichill.bordernet.co.uk
The Coldstream and District Local History Society website:
www.coldstreamhistorysociety.co.uk

Introduction

The county of Berwickshire takes its name from the town of Berwick-upon-Tweed which was part of Scotland at the time of the county's formation but finally became part of England in 1482 after centuries of Anglo-Scottish warfare. The county borders Roxburghshire and Selkirkshire to the west, East Lothian and Midlothian to the north, the North Sea (formerly called the German Ocean) to the east, and a portion of the Anglo-Scottish border to the south. It measures roughly 35 miles from east to west and 22 miles from north to south at its extremities and covers an area of 457 square miles. It can be physically divided into three districts, the largest being the fertile Merse, then the hilly and pastoral Lammermuirs and finally the smaller Lauderdale which is a mixture of hill and dale along the banks of the Leader Water.

Having lost Berwick-upon-Tweed to the English, the county was left for over a century without a head burgh until 1596 when Greenlaw was awarded the privilege, only to lose it in 1661 when the title was transferred to Duns. From 1670 Duns shared the title of County Town with Lauder, only for Greenlaw to regain the privilege in 1696. Duns made three vain attempts to regain the title before being finally successful in 1890 by virtue of the Local Government (Scotland) Act 1889 which established the system of County Councils in Scotland.

The county's principal rivers are the Tweed, the Leader, the Whiteadder, the Blackadder and the Eye, all but the latter flowing in to the Tweed which forms part of the county's southern boundary. Because of the county's location within the Borders its lands were not as prone to raids from the notorious Border reivers as were their neighbours in counties such as Selkirkshire, Roxburghshire and Dumfriesshire but they nevertheless suffered from violent incursions by English armies. This was particularly so in the sixteenth century when Scotland was politically allied to England's traditional enemy France and King Henry VIII did everything in his power to bring Scotland under his influence. When Mary, Queen of Scots, came to the throne as an infant in 1542 he had her betrothed to his son Edward to create an alliance with England but when the Scots repudiated the engagement he responded by sending armies under the Earl of Hertford in 1543 and 1544 to 'kill, burn and spoil' southern Scotland. This became known as the 'Rough Wooing' and although it was ultimately unsuccessful it resulted in many of the locations in this book being temporarily destroyed.

Although not the largest of the Border counties, Berwickshire possessed some of their largest landed estates and was home to some of the most famous and influential families in Scottish history such as the Homes, Swintons, Haigs, Hays, Maitlands, Douglasses and Trotters to name just a few. With their feudal power came responsibilities towards their servants and tenants and before the time of Old Age Pensions in 1910 there are many recorded instances of caring landowners looking after their tenants. As an example, the *Berwickshire News* in January 1877 carried a news item headed 'Seasonable Benevolence - Mrs Swinton has given fourteen tons of coal for distribution among the poor and warm clothing to the more needy recipients. Mr Alan Swinton also gives soup twice a week during the winter months'. The following year it reported that Mrs Swinton had given 21 tons of coal and that Alan Swinton had opened a public soup kitchen that had supplied 25 poor families and would continue to do so twice a week during winter.

Apart from Duns, Lauder, Coldstream and Eyemouth, there were no towns of any significant size, nor were there any significant manufacturing or mining industries so most inhabitants obtained their livelihoods by working either on the land, in domestic service or in the coastal fishing fleets. The county's large sporting estates also offered employment to many of the inhabitants.

The county has 30 miles of often spectacular coastline that stretches northwards from Berwick-upon-Tweed to the Dunglass Burn just beyond the village of Cockburnspath. There are a number of small fishing villages along its route such as Burnmouth and St Abbs but its main harbour is at Eyemouth. Nowadays a popular small holiday resort, it also has a tragic history because on 14 October 1881, the night of the 'Great Storm' along the East Coast, 20 boats which comprised most of the town's fishing fleet were lost and 129 fishermen were drowned.

The 'Great Road' from London to Edinburgh passed through the county and the first stagecoaches made the journey in 60 hours but when the Royal Mail service was introduced in 1836 it cut the journey time to 42 hours. The opening of the North British Railway Company's line between Edinburgh and Berwick-upon-Tweed in 1846 sounded the death knell for stagecoach services and the last four-horse mail coach ran from Newcastle to Edinburgh in 1847.

The town of Coldstream, which lies on the north bank of the River Tweed directly opposite Cornhill-on-Tweed in the English county of Northumberland, has a history of Border warfare and later, in the eighteenth and nineteenth centuries, was a popular centre for runaway marriages similar to Lamberton Toll on the border north of Berwick-upon-Tweed and Gretna Green on the western side of the country. However, it is best known as being the town where in 1650 General George Monck founded a regiment of Oliver Cromwell's New Model Army but ten years later marched it to London to secure the accession of King Charles II onto the English throne, thus playing a significant part in securing the continuity of the British monarchy. On 14 February 1661 the regiment symbolically laid down their arms as soldiers of the New Model Army and immediately took them up again as a Royal Regiment of Foot Guards. Following Monck's death in 1670 they adopted the name of the 'Coldstream Regiment of Foot Guards' who are nowadays known as the 'Coldstream Guards' and the 'Second Regiment of Foot'.

Allanbank House in Lauder was built by David Bryce in 1848 and appears to have had a chequered career. Its furniture was auctioned off in 1904 and the following year the house was advertised as being available to let. In November 1939 a number of evacuees from Edinburgh, whose ages ranged from two to six, were evacuated to this house under the care of a matron and her helpers. The house was later demolished and in 1945 Lauder Town Council agreed to acquire its site for housing.

This nineteenth-century lodge to Allanbank House was built in Manse Road to a Classical design with finely-channelled stonework, to which an inappropriate-looking harled rear wing was added in the twentieth century. The canted open porch to its central entrance is supported on Tuscan columns and still looks imposing although the windows either side have been modernised. Nowadays the gates have been taken away and this former drive up to the 'Big House' now gives pedestrian access to the houses on the Allanbank estate and the primary school. The tall stone gatepost on the left of the photograph is still in position but guards a road that only peters out in fields beyond a farm.

This is the front view of the house known as The Anchorage on Briery Law in the village of St Abbs near Eyemouth. From the other side of the house there is a panoramic view over Eyemouth seafront and harbour. Nowadays it is only recognisable from this picture by its castellated wing and dormer because the door and windows have all been replaced by modern ones and what appears to be an area of shiplap boards is now cemented in conformity with the rest of the building. At the time when this photograph was taken in the early 1900s, it was a boarding house run by Isabel Cowe, assisted by her slightly older sister Agnes. Isabel is the one wearing the black dress in the photograph; she was a well-known and energetic personality in the village and in 1912 was awarded the RNLI's Gold Brooch for her bravery in helping to rescue passengers from the wreck of the RMS *Glanmire*. She was also an active suffragette and in October that year took part in the suffragettes' march from Edinburgh to London in support of votes for women and, being on her bicycle, was able to leave the march at intervals to collect signatures for their petition from outlying farms and hamlets. At home in St Abbs she was renowned for standing wearing a sou'wester and carrying a hurricane lamp, pen and paper, to get the signatures of shipwrecked mariners for the suffragettes' cause. She was equally determined when it came to local affairs; on 27 January 1914 the *Berwickshire News* reported that she had refused to pay her rates to the parish council because of their irregular collections of the town's rubbish and that her household effects of a sideboard, sofa and easy chair were sold by the sheriff's officer to satisfy the debt of £1.13.11d parish rates plus 9/4d expenses. The sisters had barricaded themselves in the house but the sheriff's officer gained entry by climbing with police officers through an open balcony window. Having claimed the goods, they could only leave by forcing their way out of the kitchen door with an axe. Isobel later sold the house and bought a larger hotel called The Haven. When she died in 1931, aged 64, her ashes were scattered on its lawn and a sundial was installed there in her memory; an oak communion table was also dedicated to her memory at St Abbs Church of Scotland. Her trustees continued operating The Anchorage as a boarding house until 1945, when they sold it, and it is nowadays a private residence.

Antonshill (sometimes written as Anton's Hill), seen here in 1903, lies four and a half miles north-west of Coldstream. It was built by William Burn in 1836 in his typical style for a medium-sized two storey house. Its first family, detailed in the 1841 census, was headed by 75-year-old General Sir Martin Hunter who lived with his 65-year-old wife and his son, James Hunter, an army major on half-pay, aged 40. The household was completed by the general's three daughters and seven servants. The general had a distinguished military career, fighting in the Wars of American Independence before going on to India, Gibraltar, Trinidad and Puerto Rica. He died in 1846. Looking ahead to the 1861 census, we find the next occupants to be Matthew D. Hunter aged 57, a landed proprietor living with his 40-year-old wife Isabella and their children Martin (six years old), James (five), Isabella (four), Maria (three) and Anne (two)! They were looked after by two nurses plus a cook, house maid, laundress and a kitchen maid.

The 1881 census of Antonshill House shows quite a different scenario. By then Matthew Hunter was dead and his eldest son Martin had died in Vienna at the age of only 20, so the head of the family was 25-year-old James Hunter, a lieutenant in the 9th Lancers who had recently returned home after serving for the past two years in the Afghan war. The local celebrations on his safe return put any modern soldier's welcome reception quite into the shade. It was reported in the *Berwickshire News* that a large bonfire was lit on a neighbouring hill and refreshments were liberally provided around it. A large crowd gathered to meet his arrival at Antonshill and when his carriage arrived at the entrance gate the horses were unyoked and the crowd pulled his carriage by hand up the avenue to the house, preceded by the Swinton brass band playing the march 'Hail, the conquering hero comes'. After acknowledging the cheers of the crowd, the young man went inside to enjoy supper with a large gathering of friends and neighbours, followed by a dance that went on until well into the early hours of the morning. James is shown in the census as living with his widowed mother Isabella and his sisters Isabel, Mary, Annie and Lucy, all unmarried. The indoor staff comprised a butler, coachman, groom, lady's maid, cook, two house maids and a scullery maid. In those days, long before the creation of the Welfare State, the local gentry were expected to be munificent at Christmas time to poor people in their parish and in the 1870s and 1880s Mrs Hunter was reported in the local newspapers as having distributed warm clothing and tea and sugar to the old women of the village and giving £5 to buy coals for the poor. She was also involved in the life of Leitholm School where she regularly judged the girls' sewing classes and awarded prizes. She died in 1903 and James, who was by then a lieutenant colonel, died in 1924.

Ayton Castle.

Ayton Castle stands off the A1 London to Edinburgh road to the east of Ayton village, about five and a half miles north-west of Berwick-upon-Tweed, and this same view of the castle can best be enjoyed from the window of a train travelling along the East Coast Main Line as it sweeps round a wide curve. The original castle on this site was a pele tower that had been built by a Norman family called de Vesci. Later, it became a stronghold of the Home family but was captured and destroyed by the English in 1448. It was captured by them again in 1497 but having been subsequently restored to the Homes, it was forfeited to the crown in 1715 because of the family's involvement in the first Jacobite Rebellion. It remained in crown hands for several years until it was purchased by John Fordyce, the commissioner for lands and forests in Scotland. This family owned the estate for around 70 years and made many improvements but eventually they demolished the old tower and built a new mansion house in the Classical style in 1834 as a replacement. However, this was completely destroyed by fire before they had even taken up residence. The family went abroad and sold the estate to William Mitchell-Innes.

William Mitchell was Chief Cashier of the Bank of Scotland from 1808 to 1827. After he inherited the Parsonsgreen estate in Edinburgh he became an 'extraordinary director' of the bank in 1841 and after further inheriting the Stow estates in the Scottish Borders he hyphenated his surname to become William Mitchell-Innes. He then acquired the Ayton estates and in 1845 signed a contract with the famous architect James Gillespie Graham to build this enormous Scots Baronial fantasy in red sandstone which was completed in 1851. Following William's death at the castle in January 1860, the estate was inherited by his eldest son Alexander who immediately commissioned David Bryce to add a drawing room extension and a billiard room. Further additions were made by James Maitland Wardrop in 1864–67 and extensive internal redecoration by Bonar & Carfra in 1875 is still largely extant. The present dining room fireplace was installed in 1873 after the American author Mark Twain, who was on a Scottish tour, took a fancy to its predecessor and returned with it to the USA, where it can nowadays be seen in the Mark Twain Museum in Hartford, Connecticut. The castle is pictured here in 1907.

Alexander Mitchell-Innes married twice and his two marriages produced fifteen children. Whilst the size of Ayton Castle afforded ample room for such a large family, it also necessitated an unusually large staff to maintain it. This is evidenced by the 1861 census which shows that the 49-year-old Alexander, his 39-year-old wife and the eight children then living with them (six of them under the age of eight years) were serviced by no fewer than 24 domestic staff! These comprised a butler, two footmen, hall boy, two governesses, housekeeper, three house maids, upper nurse, two nursery maids, wet nurse, lady's maid, four laundresses, cook, kitchen maid, two scullery maids and a still room maid. In 1895 Alexander's grandson and heir of entail sold the barony, castle and lands of Ayton for £90,000 to Henry Liddell-Grainger of Middleton Hall, Northumberland, and that family owned the estate until recent times. David Liddell-Grainger died in 2007 and was buried in the estate's mausoleum which already held the bodies of two of his children. His widow Christine, Lady de la Rue, subsequently advertised the estate for sale at an asking price of £3 million and when this didn't attract prospective buyers she gained permission from Duns Sheriff Court to move the bodies from the castle's mausoleum to the village graveyard so as not to put off prospective purchasers. With a reduced asking price of £2.2 million, the castle – which comprised a main hall, inner hall, gallery, drawing room, dining room, library, boudoir, small dining room, breakfasting kitchen, billiard room, domestic offices, seventeen bedrooms and nine bathrooms – was eventually sold in 2014 to Richard Syred and Brian Parsons.

Ayton Castle West Lodge, seen here in 1907, matched the castle in its Scots Baronial style. Its red sandstone archway and screen walls are seen at their best in the rays of the evening sun.

Two views of Ayton Castle's extensive grounds with the rock garden pictured in 1923 and the Ladies' Bridge in 1897.

Balabraes House at Ayton was the home of Sir Walter Grindlay Simpson, Bart., who was born in 1843 and died in 1898. He was a close friend of Robert Louis Stevenson and was a patron and founder-member of the nine-hole Ayton Golf Club which existed from 1891 to 1928. His interest in the game was such that in 1892 he published a book called *The Art of Golf*. His father, the first baronet, was Sir James Young Simpson (1811–1870) who was an obstetrician famous for discovering the anaesthetic properties of chloroform and introducing it for general medical use.

BALABRAES, AYTON.

Situated off the A6089 road about two miles north-west of Gordon, Bassendean has been the seat of the Homes of Bassendean since 1583. Only a fragment of the original tower house on the site remains; it was replaced by this three-storey house which was built in the seventeenth century with later additions. The greenhouse on the left of the picture was built onto one of the remaining tower house walls during the nineteenth century but was removed in the mid-twentieth century, and turrets were added to the original fifteen-foot-high walls to bring it up to the height of the rest of the house. In the seventeenth century George Home of Bassendean, who was a committed Protestant during the reign of the Catholic King James II, was hounded by the state for his beliefs; he escaped to Holland and was one of the nobles who masterminded the 'Glorious Revolution' which brought King William of Orange and Queen Mary to the British throne in 1689. A later incumbent was John Hutcheson Fergusson who took the name Home on inheriting the estate of Bassendean in 1860. Previous to that, at the age of 28 and an officer in the Indian Army in Bengal, he had married 24-year-old Jane Anne Walker in Edinburgh in 1851 but she died in India the following year and was buried there. The 1861 census for Bassendean shows him to be living in the mansion and described as a 47-year-old retired Major of the 33rd Regiment, Bengal Native Infantry, together with his second wife, 27-year-old Dorothea Veitch who he had married earlier that year, and employing only three domestic servants. The couple were still there at the time of the 1881 census and were now employing only two domestic servants for their mansion – extremely frugal compared with many other landowners. The house at that time comprised a hall, lobby, drawing room, dining room, seven bedrooms, pantries, kitchen, laundry and the conservatory. John died in 1881 and Dorothea in 1888; both are buried in the Dean Cemetery in Edinburgh.

Belchester House is situated about five miles north-west of Coldstream and is south-east of the village of Leitholm. The estate had been the seat of the Dickson family from the fourteenth century and the house was built sometime about 1800 around a pele tower core. When it was first built, the house was probably U-shaped with the two arms facing south but in the 1830s substantial additions were made that included the construction of a fourth wing. This created a central courtyard which was then roofed over to form a much larger house. In the later part of the twentieth century a service wing and conical tower were demolished. In 1715 James Dickson of Belchester participated in the unsuccessful Jacobite uprising of that year and had to flee to America but lived to return home safely. In 1797 the last Dickson to own the estate married Jane, the daughter of Sir Martin Hunter GCMG, GCH, of Medomsley, County Durham and Antons Hill, County Berwick, and the estate subsequently passed out of the family's hands.

Bemersyde is a country house lying one and three-quarter miles north-east of Newtown St Boswells and close to the River Tweed. The house incorporates a rectangular tower dating back to 1535 which was destroyed by the English during their raids in 1547; it was rebuilt in 1580 and lower wings were added in the eighteenth century to the west and east. These wings on either side of the tower originally matched. The east wing, built in 1796, remains as was intended when built but the west, built earlier in 1761, has been altered at least twice; its height was raised considerably by extra storeys being added but one of these was later removed. The central tower itself rises to five storeys and, as it dates from the early sixteenth century, it was probably built in conformity with the Act of the Scots Parliament in 1535 'for bigging of strengthis on the Bordouris'. Its walls reach a thickness of ten feet and the tower may well incorporate portions of an earlier house in its foundations. The upper storey is a seventeenth-century reconstruction, built in 1690 with stone salvaged from the ruins of Dryburgh Abbey. Further alterations in 1841 and 1859 (the replacement of the west wing) were followed by alterations in 1923 by J.P. Alison & Hobkirk of Hawick.

Bemersyde House was originally built to protect the Monks' Ford which lay virtually equidistant between Dryburgh Abbey and Old Melrose Abbey and the Haig family have possessed the land since a Norman knight, Petrus del Hage, built a castle here. The direct line of the family died out in 1867 and the ancestral manor passed into other Haig hands (the distillers' branch) but in 1921 the nation purchased the manor from a cousin and presented it to Sir Douglas Haig who in 1919 had been created Earl Haig, Viscount of Dawick and Baron Haig of Bemersyde House, as a reward for his services as Commander in Chief of British Forces during the Great War. Towards the end of the thirteenth century Thomas the Rhymer had made the prophecy that 'Tyde what may betide / Haig shall be Haig of Bemersyde' and the house is still the seat of Clan Haig. The gardens were laid out by Earl Haig and are open to the public.

The castle on this site was destroyed in the early 1500s by an English army commanded by the Earl of Surrey and its remains were probably incorporated into this magnificent eighteenth-century Blackadder House. There were more than two centuries of intrigue and warfare between the Blackadder family and the Homes but in 1671 Sir John Home was created Baronet of Blackadder and the Homes retained the estate until 1836. Around the mid 1700s James Playfair drew up plans for the castle to be substantially rebuilt and remodelled; these plans came to nothing but in 1784 the building was extended and castellated by Robert Adam. The estate, which is near the village of Allanton, was purchased from the Homes in 1836 by General Sir William Houstoun, the first Baronet of Calderhall, and he was succeeded in 1842 by his eldest son, Sir George Augustus Frederick Houstoun, who added Boswall to his name in 1847 when he married Euphemia Boswall. Around 1840 a magnificent conservatory was built in the manner of a Gothic chapel with a framework made entirely of cast iron and with some of the glass panels stained, all at a cost of several thousand pounds. Sometime around 1853 the house was further remodelled and extended by John Lessels who added a large asymmetrical wing and balustraded the terraces, the finished structure being a large classical house built in the Palladian style. This view is of the front of the house which is much less ornate than the back.

The magnificent rear view of Blackadder House which had an establishment to match. The 1871 census lists retired colonel Sir George Augustus Frederick Houstoun-Boswall, Bart., 2nd Baronet of Calderhall, aged 61, plus his wife Euphemia, aged 52, and their son Thomas, aged 20. Their domestic staff comprised a butler, under-butler, lady's maid, cook, three house maids, laundry maid, under-laundry maid, diary maid, kitchen maid, scullery maid and two footmen. Moving forward several years the 4th Baronet was Captain Sir George Reginald Houstoun-Boswall who married Miss Naomi Anstey in 1913. He had already fought in the Boer War and then went off to fight again on the outbreak of the First World War, but died at the Battle of Loos in 1915, leaving Naomi with a young baby named Phoebe. Naomi inherited the estate and the baronetcy passed to her brother-in-law, Randolph. To make matters worse the house was requisitioned by the government to be used as accommodation for troops who vandalised the building to the extent of even using parts of the grand staircase banister for firewood. The post-war government refused to pay for the restitution of the house to its pre-war condition, the family didn't have the money to do it and Naomi had had enough. In 1922 she moved into a magnificent house in Cornwall Terrace overlooking London's Regent's Park, which she named Boswall House, and put the Blackadder estate up for sale.

The contents of Blackadder House were sold by Wylie & Lochead of Glasgow at a public auction held in the house on 15–17 October 1924 and in the same year the estate of around 5,000 acres was sold to Mr W.E. Towler. The house itself was purchased for demolition by Charles Brand, a contractor of Dundee who had already carried out similar work on unwanted Scottish mansions. In the early part of 1925 a notice was published in the *Southern Reporter* headed *Demolition of Blackadder House, Berwickshire. For sale at the above job* and it listed, amongst other items, 'Large Quantities of Building Stone, Stone Paving, Stone Flagging, Scotch Slates, Wood and Stone Balustrades, Flooring, Joists, Rafters, Cast Iron Palisading, 2 Large Stone Fountain Beds, 2 Old Stone Pillars with Sundial Top, Large Entrance Gates, 100 Doors, 150 Windows, Oak Framed French Windows with Mirrored Shutters, Carved Oak Fitment of Doors, Pine Staircase, Valuable Mantelpieces and Grates, Stone and Marble Shelving. Apply to Foreman or C. Brand'. One wonders where some of these items ended up and whether they still grace various homes.

These imposing gates and pillars at the entrance to Blackadder House, pictured here in 1913, were amongst the items sold when the house was demolished in 1925. They were purchased by Alderman William Duncan of Morpeth and re-erected as the entrance to the Formal Gardens section of Carlisle Park in Morpeth where they proudly stand to this day.

This house, named Bonardub, was built in 1901 on Eyemouth Road in Coldingham by the Simpson family and is still owned by them. In its early days a frequent visitor was Edinburgh-born Evelyn Blantyre Simpson (1855–1920), the daughter of Sir James Young Simpson who popularised the use of chloroform as an anaesthetic. A good example is in the summer of 1904 when the *Berwickshire News & General Advertiser* frequently reported that amongst the visitors to Coldingham were 'Miss Simpson, party and maids'. Evelyn (actually christened 'Eve') wrote biographies both of her father and Robert Louis Stevenson, who was a close family friend, and also a book on Scottish folklore.

The foundation stone of Bonkyl Lodge at the east end of the village of Preston was laid by Lady Dunglass on 14 January 1878. It was built as a residence for the Hon. George Douglas-Home (brother of the 12th Earl of Home) and in November the following year the *Berwickshire News & General Advertiser* reported that the handsome shooting lodge being erected by Lord Dunglass was almost completed at a cost of around £6,000 and comprised a drawing room, dining room, library and kitchen on the ground floor with bedrooms and dressing rooms on the upper floor. The 1901 census shows that the household comprised of George Douglas-Home, aged 47, and his elder sister Elizabeth, aged 56, together with a butler, footman, lady's maid, cook, two house maids, diary maid and a kitchen maid. This photograph dates from 1905.

Broad Meadows is situated in Hutton where most of the land was once owned by the Ker family of Broadmeadows who acted as baillies for the Homes. In 1803 the estate passed into the ownership of the Swintons of Kimmerghame who held it until 1825 when it became the property of Mr Joseph MacBraire. The mansion was built around 1811 and was probably designed by the architect David Hamilton. Its frontage was built in a Grecian style using white coloured sandstone. The estate was sold and broken up in 1914 when the house and home farm were sold to Mr J. Watts who demolished the greater part of the house around 1915 and remodelled the rest. In 1923 the house and farm were sold to Mr John William Stewart. It has since had a number of owners and is nowadays a working farm with five self-catering cottages in its 400-acre grounds.

Broom House at Edrom was built by Colonel James Home in 1813 on the site of, and incorporating the walls of, an old pele tower and several skeletons were discovered when digging its foundations. The colonel was unmarried and was succeeded in 1849 by his nephew, Colonel George Logan, who was born in 1803 and died in 1870. He became the 12th Laird of Broomhouse and assumed the name of Home. The 1861 census shows the household to comprise George Logan Home, aged 55, his wife Anne Doran, aged 38, and their sons William James, aged thirteen, George John Ninian, aged six, and daughter Helen, aged one, complete with a nursery maid, butler, coachman, groom, cook, house maid, laundry maid and diary maid. Of the two sons William became a lieutenant in the Royal Engineers but died at Simla in India aged only 28, whilst George, the 13th Laird, married Eva Seton in 1878 and died in 1936. The family's seat was Edrom House and they eventually decided to sell Broom House; in the early 1970s it was described as being a ruin and was demolished before the end of that decade, its Adam chimneypiece now gracing the Music Room in Edrom House.

The Charterhall estate near Greenlaw has belonged to the Trotter family since the 1600s. They were a Lowland clan who had supported the Royalist and the early Jacobite causes; in earlier years their chief had been killed in 1513 fighting the English at Flodden. The Edinburgh architect John Lessels designed this house in 1852 and also its South Lodge and stables in 1865. The stables are built of cream sandstone masonry and are arranged around a square courtyard. Cottages are incorporated into the west range and there is a further cottage to the right of the stables that would once have served as the groom's house. The stables are still in use and their interior contains some original features. The nineteenth-century house shown here was demolished and replaced in 1966 by a modern house which is owned by Major and Mrs Trotter and is situated south of the Blackadder Water and to the east of Charterhall Wood, adjacent to the site of the old house.

Another view of Charterhall House. Major-General Sir Henry Trotter of the Grenadier Guards, who commanded the Brigade of Guards and the Home District for a number of years, directed the military arrangements for Queen Victoria's funeral and King Edward VII's coronation. He was born in 1844 and was the 11th Baronet of Mortonhall, Midlothian (the family seat), and the 2nd of Charterhall, Berwickshire. In 1866 he married Eva Gifford, the eldest daughter of the second Lord Gifford and had four sons, all of whom saw service on the front line during the Boer War. He was appointed chief staff officer to the Duke of Connaught who was in supreme command of the troops at King Edward's coronation in 1902. That same year General Trotter became furious when Westminster Council provided its street workers, including dustmen and scavengers, with uniforms and caps similar to those worn by the Guards. He wrote in protest and the colour of the caps was changed because they really did look almost identical to those of the Guards! He retired from the army in 1904 and died the following year, aged sixty-one.

Clint Lodge stands on the B6356 road at Clintmains, north-east of St Boswells, and was built in 1869 by Lord Polwarth as the family's shooting home on part of the Duke of Sutherland's estate. This picture shows the house in the early years of the twentieth century with the entrance gate quite close to the front of the house. The house has been a small luxury hotel since 1997; the gate and trees have gone and the curving wall has been realigned with the road to give a wider space in front of the entrance, which is approached by a driveway out of sight to the right of the picture.

COCKBURNSPATH TOWER.

Cockburnspath (locally pronounced Co'path) Tower is a ruined late-fifteenth/early-sixteenth-century tower house with later outbuildings in a courtyard entered by an arched gateway. Situated south-east of the village of the same name just below a viaduct on the A1 road from Edinburgh to Berwick, it stands above a steep-sided ravine overlooking the Tower Burn. The keep is rectangular in plan and stands at the north-west corner of a courtyard which once enclosed a range of ancillary buildings. It measures approximately eleven feet by nine feet and its walls are on average six feet thick.

Originally it was four storeys high and probably had a parapet walk around the top. Today the north wall remains to a height of around eleven feet and shows evidence of doors and windows in it. The recorded history of a castle at Cockburnspath goes back to 1073 when it was owned by the Earls of Dunbar and March and remained in their possession until the time of the 11th Earl of March when in 1435 their lands were forfeited and returned to the crown. Twenty year later the Scottish King James II made his second son, Alexander Stewart (who was already titled Duke of Albany), the Earl of March and granted him the lands of the earldom including the castle and barony of Cockburnspath. The castle pictured here probably dates from this period. However, in 1503 they formed part of the dowry paid by King James IV on his marriage to Margaret Tudor but following his death at Flodden in 1513 Margaret married Archibald Douglas, 6th Earl of Angus (the 'Red' Douglas), in the following year and he claimed the barony of Cockburnspath in her name.

This began a dispute with Archibald's brother-in-law, John Home of Blackadder, which the Homes eventually won and they took possession of Cockburnspath Tower. The tower and barony changed hands a number of times during the period of the 'Rough Wooing' but it was owned by the Homes until 1682 when it was bought by Sir John Hall who was later created 1st Baronet of Dunglass. The times now became more peaceable following the Union of the Crowns in 1707 and the defensive tower fell out of regular use. By the late eighteenth century it was being used as a source of stone for local building work and the site became very overgrown with trees growing out of the masonry and destabilising the stonework. In the winter of 2011/12 a massive section of walling (on the nearside of the picture) at second floor level collapsed and a huge pile of its rubble now lies at the base of the tower.

Coveyheugh House has been described as a Georgian/Victorian mansion but the author hasn't been able to trace its history or its residents earlier than the 1850s. It stands on the Grantshouse side of the village of Reston and the view eastwards from its terrace encompasses the Lammermuir Hills and the valley of the Eye Water. Sometime around 1855 Thomas Montgomery, minister of the United Presbyterian Chapel at neighbouring Ayton, moved into the house because the 1861 census shows him, aged 38, living there with his wife Agnes, 34, and their two sons and four daughters aged ten, nine, seven, five and three years old plus a baby. The family can't have stayed there for very long because the occupants in the 1871 census were Thomas Anderson, aged 64, a landed proprietor and farmer who previously lived at Shawbraes, together with his wife, older unmarried sister, son, two daughters, a house maid, a kitchen maid and two farm servants. They in turn only stayed for a few years because in 1874 the estate was purchased by James Smith Mack. Born in Edinburgh in 1825 he became a successful lawyer and for many years he commuted daily in summer from Reston Junction railway station to Edinburgh Waverley station, returning in the late afternoon, a round trip of 92 miles. The 1881 census sees him at the height of his career, aged 55: a justice of the peace, a deputy lieutenant of Berwickshire, a notary public and a solicitor before the supreme courts! He was living with his wife Hughina, daughter Mary, son James and a cook, table maid and house maid. He was also a deeply religious man and very involved in church and civic affairs. But all these responsibilities took a toll on his health and by the time of the 1901 census the table maid had been replaced by a sick nurse.

James Smith Mack of Coveyheugh House died in 1903, only eight weeks after his wife's death, and very shortly an advertisement appeared in the *Berwickshire News & General Advertiser* announcing that an auction would be held in Coveyheugh House of 'Substantial Household Furnishings, Plate, (Grand) Pianoforte, Organ, Bookcase, Books, Pictures and Other Miscellaneous Effects'. The principal rooms in the house were a hall, drawing room, dining room, library and seven bedrooms. It was subsequently purchased by Archibald Baird MRCVS who practised as a veterinary surgeon in Edinburgh and was a major in the Army Veterinary Corps during the Great War.

He died at Coveyheugh in 1939 at the age of 81. The house is currently the home of the Institute of Colon Hydrotherapy but was advertised for sale in 2015 with an asking price of £550,000. Its outward appearance is virtually unchanged from these 1909 pictures but, alas, the stylish greenhouse is no more.

Cranshaws Castle, Cranshaws.

Cranshaws Castle originated as a pele tower that was probably built in the late fifteenth or early sixteenth century and was originally a stronghold of the Douglas family. In 1401 the tower and lands of the Cranshaws were acquired by the Swintons by a grant from Archibald, 4th Earl of Douglas. They are thought to have built this elegant round-cornered five-storey tower house in the late sixteenth century. It is situated in the Lammermuir Hills about nine miles north-west of Duns off the B6356 road and measures 40 feet by 26 feet on the ground and 65 feet to the parapet. The Swintons had kept it in fairly good repair but in 1702 they sold it to David Denham, in whose ownership it fell into disrepair but remained habitable. His son sold it to James Watson of Saughton in 1739 and it descended through his mother to George Douglas, Lord Aberdour, who was the eldest son of the Earl of Morton. Several repairs and improvements were carried out between 1773 and 1815 and in 1895 the castle was bought by Andrew Smith of Whitchester who restored it in 1896–97.

It became the property of his grand-nephew in 1931 and is still owned and occupied by his family, the Landales. The castle, pictured here in 1923, is thought to have been the inspiration for Ravenswood Castle which was the home of the hero, Edgar, in Sir Walter Scott's tragic novel *The Bride of Lammermoor*. Since late 2015 the castle has been available as a holiday let costing from £1,000 per night.

Dryburgh House is a Scottish Baronial-style house dating back to 1845 when it was the home of Lady Griselle Baillie. In 1875 it was modernised by her brother, Lord Jerviswoode, and remained in the family until 1929 when it was purchased by the Scottish Motor Traction Company who added the east wing and launched it as a 'Tourist Hotel' in 1932. The hotel changed hands a number of times over the years until 2007 when it was taken over by a company who re-launched it as the luxurious Dryburgh Abbey Hotel. It stands in a ten-acre estate on the banks of the River Tweed adjacent to the ruins of Dryburgh Abbey, the burial place of Sir Walter Scott.

Dryburgh House

The history of Duns Castle stretches back for many centuries. The land was granted by King Robert the Bruce to his nephew Randolph, Earl of Moray, in 1320 and he built the original castle as an L-plan pele tower which measured 50 feet by 35 feet with a projecting 30-foot-square wing and walls eight feet thick; this now forms part of the tower at the east end of the building. There were many changes of ownership over the next three centuries but in 1696 the Earl of Tweeddale purchased the lands of Duns and Crumstane for his son, William Hay of Drummelzier, at a cost of £228,034.14.3d Scots (£19,002.17.10d Sterling) and the Hay family have lived there in unbroken succession ever since. William Hay's wife was a descendent of Mary Seton who was a lady-in-waiting to Mary, Queen of Scots, and one of the 'Four Marys' who always attended her. Over the years the family have enlarged and improved the castle and its present form is the work of the famous architect James Gillespie Graham between 1818 and 1822. In earlier days General Leslie used the castle for his quarters during the Scottish Covenanters' uprising against King Charles I in 1639.

A mansion of the size of Duns Castle needed a domestic establishment to match. The 1871 census for the castle shows the family in residence to have been the owner, William Hay, aged 83, his son William James, aged 43 and long retired from service in India, unmarried daughters Christian, 47, and Harriet, 43, married daughters Ann, 45, and Cordelia, 41, plus two grandsons and four granddaughters. The domestic staff comprised a valet, lady's maid, nurse, nursery governess, housekeeper, house maid, two under-house maids, table maid, cook, kitchen maid, laundry maid and under-laundry maid. There would almost certainly have been a butler employed as well. This view of the castle looks across the artificial lake that was created from a glacial drainage channel when the Hay family landscaped the grounds of Duns Castle in the eighteenth century. The lake is known locally as the Heron Pond ('Hen Poo' in the Scots vernacular) and it is nowadays a nature reserve that provides a feeding and breeding ground for wildfowl.

At the other end of the town the road from the town centre to Duns Castle passes from Castle Street firstly through the gateway of the North Lodge and then, a little further along, through the Pavilion Lodge pictured here with its tall Gothic archway spanning the road and its flanking castellated towers. It was built in the late 1770s by John Baxter junior and added to in 1791. It is nowadays used as a self-catering holiday cottage.

Approaching Duns along the A6105 road from Greenlaw one comes to the South Lodge entrance to Duns Castle which has long been known as 'Sally's Lodge' after a former keeper who lived here in the lodge on the left of the tower. The lodge itself, which was built around 1820, is almost hidden in this picture behind trees and bushes with only its window visible. Equally well hidden is a smaller square tower behind the creeper on the other side of the arch. A camp for 300 Polish soldiers was situated here during the Second World War. Today almost all of the creeper has gone and the lodge has a very smart appearance.

The next four pictures are appropriate to Duns Castle and its environment more than a century ago. There is no established link between these photographs and the castle (they may possibly have been taken at Manderston House) but they were taken by a Duns photographer somewhere in the area, probably in the 1880s or 1890s, and show contrasting images of the lives of the gentry and their servants in those days. On this page, the languid upper-class family wearing hats are relaxing on the steps of their mansion with their dogs whilst the groom, wearing a cap, holds the lady's horse ready for her to mount. She appears to be the same lady in the next photograph, sitting side-saddle, which is not as uncomfortable or precarious as it looks. All upper-class ladies rode in this way and hunting must have called for exceptionally fine horsemanship when jumping fences and ditches.

In complete contrast to the privileged lives of the subjects on the previous page we have the pictures of a housekeeper and her staff, all unmarried ladies of varying ages and carrying the tools of their trade, as are the eight gardeners necessary to maintain their mansion's extensive grounds.

Eccles House was built between 1895 and 1898 for James Lewis Greig and replaced an earlier house that was situated a short distance to the north. It was designed by the Edinburgh architect Thomas Greenshields Leadbetter in the seventeenth-century Scottish Revival style and is built of sandstone and painted harl with both Venetian and pedimented windows, whilst the interior contains a number of Art Nouveau features. It is said that the stable block was built by a previous owner, Sir John Paterson, out of money he won from the Duke of Roxburghe at the card table. The clock in the stable tower marks the time with only a single hand and, as such, is said to be unique in Scotland.

Rosary & Nunnery. Eccles House.

This picture shows the few remaining parts of the Convent Church of St Mary the Virgin which is situated in the grounds of Eccles House. This was a nunnery which is believed to have been founded sometime between 1145 and 1156 by Cospatrick Home, 3rd Earl of Dunbar, and was consecrated to the Virgin Mary. The nunnery paid homage to Kings Edward I, II and III in order to obtain protection against the English armies but in 1545 the Earl of Hertford, on a two-day raid into Scotland, destroyed both the village and its nunnery. The convent grounds are thought to have covered an area of around six acres but the baptismal font and ruins on the left of this 1911 picture are all that remain of the convent buildings and consist of the barrel-vaulted ground floor and fragments of carved columns and walls that have been incorporated into a modern garden wall. The building in the centre of the picture is a summerhouse.

Eccles Lodge

This lodge was built in the mid-nineteenth century to serve the original Eccles House which was replaced at the end of that century by the newer house in the previous pictures. Its doorway is entered through the porch which is supported on paired columns and happily this scene on the main road through Eccles appears exactly the same today as in this 1907 photograph.

EDROM HOUSE, BERWICKSHIRE

Standing at the western edge of Edrom village the mansion of Edrom House was built in 1740 in a style that was already considered old-fashioned for its time. It was later extended when a two-storey rear wing was added around 1774, followed by a single-storey music room in 1908 which has an Adam chimneypiece taken from the now-demolished Broom House. The mansion was described in 1846 as being 'beautifully situated, commanding some very rich scenery, with distant views of the hills of Dunse [Duns] and Cockburn and the Lammermuir and Cheviot Hills'. There is an interesting contrast between the two pictures: in the first the creeper covers the whole of the frontage and the music room has a flat roof, whereas in the second, more recent one, the creeper on the front of the house only extends to the right of the doorway and the music room has a pitched roof. The music room appears unchanged today but the creeper has now disappeared altogether. With eight bedrooms, four reception rooms, a library and even a priest-hole plus 20 acres of land, it has been the home of supermodel Stella Tennant and her immediate family since 2002.

Fast Castle lies four and a half miles north-west of the village of Coldingham and overlooks the North Sea with cliffs up to 148 feet high surrounding the promontory. It once comprised a courtyard and keep, surrounded by a curtain wall with towers, but apart from the section of the north-east wall shown in the picture nothing remains of the other buildings except their foundations. It was approached by a very steep path that led to a drawbridge over a 24-foot-wide chasm and a guidebook of 1829 warned that 'Great care is required not to slip or fall in descending as a false step might hurry the unwary traveller by one projection into the boiling deep below'. The castle changed hands many times during centuries of Border warfare. It was first recorded in 1333 and in 1346 the site was occupied by an English garrison who used it as a base for pillaging the surrounding countryside but in 1410 it was recaptured by a Scottish force led by Patrick Dunbar, the second son of the tenth Earl of Dunbar and March. The castle later fell into the hands of the Homes and in 1503 they hosted Margaret Tudor, daughter of the English King Henry VII, who was on her way to Scotland to marry King James IV. But the king and numerous Homes were killed at the Battle of Flodden in 1513 and afterwards a feud broke out between that family and the Regent Albany in which the latter came out the winner. The castle was destroyed in 1515, Alexander Home was executed in 1516 and his lands were forfeited, only to be restored to the family by 1522 when the castle was rebuilt by George, the 4th Lord Home.

The English captured Fast Castle again in 1547 during the period of the 'Rough Wooing' but it was back in Homes' hands by 1566 when Mary, Queen of Scots, stayed there. The castle then passed to Sir Robert Logan of Restalrig through his mother, a widow of Lord Home. He was a very shady character and after his death in 1606 it was found that he had been involved in the 'Gowie Conspiracy' whereby the young King James VI was intended to be kidnapped and held captive at Fast Castle by his enemies who were loyal to the English Queen Elizabeth I. His corpse was exhumed in 1609, brought into court and put on trial for high treason! His estates were forfeited and his children were outlawed but whilst the latter punishment was rescinded in 1613 the titles and estates were never restored to the family. By this time the castle was in a ruinous state. It passed briefly to the Douglas family, then back to the Earls of Dunbar, then to the family of Arnot, then back to the Homes and finally in 1683 to Sir John Hall, Baronet of Dunglass, whose family held it until 1919 when it was acquired by Mr Frank Usher, along with the Dunglass estate which they still own. The castle was used by Sir Walter Scott as the model for the keep of 'Wolf's Crag', the home of the young Master of Ravenswood and his faithful seneschal, Caleb Balderstone, in the tragic novel *The Bride of Lammermoor*.

Situated three miles east of Melrose in the parish of Mertoun the early-nineteenth-century single-storey pavilion house of Gladswood was possibly built by Andrew Naysmyth. In the late nineteenth century it was the seat of the Meiklam family who held 258 acres in the parish. Queen Victoria stopped here in August 1867 as she was driving from Melrose to Floors Castle. The family at that time consisted of John Meiklam, a landed proprietor aged 58, together with his wife Mary, aged 57, and his unmarried daughter Julia, aged 37. Also living in the house were their coachman, footman, lady's maid, housekeeper, house maid, two kitchen maids and a scullery maid.

The lands of Greenknowe were obtained by the Setons in the early fifteenth century when Alexander Seton married a Gordon heiress. Greenknowe Tower was built in 1581 by James Seton of Touch at the time he married his second wife, Jane Edmonstone. This date and their monograms are carved on the lintel above the front door. The tower stands on a knoll to the west of Gordon village and was originally defended by marshy surroundings. L-plan in shape, the main block measures 23 feet by 35 feet with walls four feet thick and is built in red sandstone topped by corbelled angle turrets and crowstepped gables. The entrance to the vaulted ground floor, which housed the kitchen and was also used for storage, is defended with an iron yett but the four floors above it are open to the sky. The great hall was on the first floor and the family lived on the three floors above it. In 1637 the Setons sold the estate to Walter Pringle whose son, Walter Pringle of Stichel, a noted Covenanter, lived there later in that century and it may have been he who refurbished the tower, enlarging the windows on the upper floors and adding an extension to the north side, later demolished. In 1720 the tower and estates passed to Adam Faiholm through his marriage to Isobel Pringle and then in 1840 the estates were sold to the Dalrymple family. The tower had been derelict since at least 1830 but was extensively repaired around 1937 before the Dalrymples passed it into the care of Historic Scotland.

Harryburn House is a fine country house that lies to the east of the A68 road just north of Lauder and close to the Harry Burn. It was built in 1827 for John Romanes, a banker and town clerk of Lauder, to designs by John Smith (1782–1864) who later added the Regency-style balconies supported on slim columns to the main house in 1851; the entire house was built wholly in the local dark whinstone with sandstone dressings. The 1851 census shows 62-year-old John living with his 45-year-old wife Isabella and their four sons, two daughters and two servants. Ten years later John's eldest son Robert, aged 34 and a solicitor, was now head of the household and this remained the case until his death in 1898. His wife Anne died in 1902 and the house remained occupied by his unmarried daughters Helen and Isabella. Helen died in 1908 aged 74 and Isabella continued alone, aided by a cook and three maids, until her death in 1932 aged 85. The house was then purchased by Mr and Mrs James Marshall but their occupation was brief. There is a reference in July 1945 to the house being the Women's Land Army Lauder Hostel but in May 1946 an announcement was made in the local press that the house was being sold by direction of the Earl and Countess of Lauderdale with vacant possession. It was described as being modernised with nine bedrooms, three reception rooms, three bathrooms, central heating and electric light. Standing in fifteen acres of its own ground, it was also described as a residential, agricultural estate and handy for hunting with the Lauderdale and the Buccleuch hounds. The latter attractions cannot have appealed to prospective purchasers because in 1948 it was advertised in the papers as being 'a family guest house run for a family' and by 1952 its facilities included radio, electric fires and hot and cold water in all bedrooms. But that was a long time ago and today the property is once again a private house.

The lodge at the entrance to the driveway to Harryburn House, possibly built by John Smith in 1855, has always been known colloquially as Chuckie Lodge because of the coursed river pebbles (or 'chuckies') that are such a prominent feature of its construction. The two pierced gate piers with pyramidal caps and finials and the gates with anthemion details are both of cast-iron but the railings with fleur-de-lys heads flanking the gateposts are of wrought-iron. This picture shows the lodge as it appeared around 1912; nowadays officially called Chuckie Lodge it is still easily recognisable because the gateway and the porch are unchanged although one of the chimney stacks has gone, the windows are modern and a small extension has been built onto the rear.

In 1611 the 1st Earl of Home contracted to buy the Hirsel estate from Sir John Ker but it wasn't until 1621 that King James VI finally granted the lands to the 2nd Earl. The Homes moved into the Hirsel after their main residence, Hume Castle, was destroyed by Cromwellian forces in 1651. Situated on a terrace above the Leet valley, the main part of the house, with its square corner towers, is of the 1670s but between 1739–41 William Adam added a new wing and built offices and courtyard walls for the 8th Earl of Home. Internally there is a very fine Restoration staircase modelled after the one at Holyrood House and further alterations and additions were made between 1813 and 1818 by William Atkinson and William Burn, including the fine central hall. Yet more alterations were made in 1858 by David Bryce and later by James C. Walker. In 1832 Cospatrick Alexander Home, the 11th Earl, married Lady Lucy Elizabeth Montague Douglas whose antecedents went back to the twelfth century, being descended from William Douglas who is widely acknowledged as the founder of the 'Black' Douglas family and their estates. The two families and their estates came together and they carried out further extensive improvements to the estate buildings and the Hirsel policies. Cospatrick died in 1881 and his successor made further improvements between 1895 and 1900 including the erection of a new wing to the house, and a chapel (both removed in 1958–59) and the building of the stables. In 1902 the thirteenth Earl of Home married Lillian Lambton, daughter of the Earl of Durham, and so cemented an alliance across the Border. Their son Alexander was born in 1903 and, as Lord Dunglass, played first-class cricket for Middlesex and the MCC. He was elected to Parliament in 1931 and served as Private Parliamentary Secretary to Neville Chamberlain at the time the latter was attempting to avert a second world war. On his father's death in 1951 he became the 14th Earl of Home and served in the House of Lords as Foreign Secretary in Harold Macmillan's government but when the latter resigned in 1963 he renounced his peerage and, as Sir Alec Douglas-Home, became Prime Minister until the General Election of 1964. He held the post of Foreign Secretary again between 1970 and 1974, after which he returned to the House of Lords as Lord Home of the Hirsel, and he died in 1995 aged 92. The present (2015) holder of the title is David Alexander Cospatrick Douglas-Home, the 15th Earl of Home.

The Hirsel's handsome stable block, built of red sandstone and crowstepped, stands a little way from the house and was built around 1900. This picture shows it soon after it was built.

The 'Blaeberry Bower' in the grounds of the Hirsel.

This footbridge spans the fast-flowing Leet Water which passes below the rear of the house and is part of a popular public walk through the Hirsel estate.

Indian Cattle grazing on the Hirsel estate. A semi-subterranean cow-arch was built in the parkland so that the operation of herding livestock under the drive towards the dairy (built *c.* 1900) is screened from the view of occupants of the house.

The impressive laundry, which was built in 1890 to service the Hirsel, has a stone base and half-timbered upper floor. It is nowadays divided into three properties. The equally impressive dairy can be seen in the background.

This quite impressive family house named Hope Park in Duns Road, Coldstream, with south facing views to the Cheviots, was built in 1874 for Thomas Hogg who ran a business as a seedsman. The house was built with a hall, dining room, drawing room, study, lounge, four reception rooms and nine bedrooms. Its panelled entrance door is framed by Tuscan columns with pilasters supporting the cornice and internally its reception rooms retain their moulded cornices and roses. There is a stained glass window on the stairwell displaying the date of 1874

and the initials 'TH' (for Thomas Hogg) with a cast-iron balustrade to the hall staircase. The two and a half acres also included a stone-built coach house, stable and tack room and a separate walled garden. The first census after Hogg moved into his new house was in 1881 when he was recorded as a 59-year-old unmarried seedsman with 60 acres and employing six men, four boys, two women and two girls. His domestic staff comprised only a housekeeper and a house maid. Visitors on the night of the census were Sarah Mason, 32, and Elizabeth Lawson, 56. Ten years later in the 1891 census he had become a Justice of the Peace with a live-in cook and a house maid, together with visitors Mary M. Cochran aged nineteen and, again, Elizabeth Lawson, now 66 (was she more than just a visitor?). However, by the time of the 1901 census everything had changed. The head of the household was now Agnes Jane Rodger, aged 74, who was Thomas's widowed sister, together with his brother Alexander W. Hogg, aged 67, and nephew Alexander, a 28-year-old medical student born in New Zealand. The household was complemented by a cook, a table maid, and Amy Tennant, aged 24, born in Australia and described here as a 'companion'. The house is currently divided into two separate properties with the four-bedroom wing run as a holiday let but in 2015 the entire estate was offered for sale at a price of in excess of £725,000.

The Houndwood estate had originally formed part of the estates of Coldingham Priory and the oldest part of Houndwood House is thought to date from the 1500s. It is accessed from the A1 road between Reston and Grantshouse by a long driveway and over the centuries has been owned by, among others, the Home, Turnbull and Coulson families. Its architecture has also evolved over the centuries and major reconstruction work was carried out in the 1840s when its front was redesigned and seventeenth-century-style baronial crowsteps were added. Internally there was a hall, dining room, drawing room, library and seven bedrooms. The sitting room still has an Adam fireplace and there is an open fireplace and ornate plaster work in the dining room. This picture is dated 1905, before the house was further extensively enlarged and modernised a few years later. It stands in 22 acres of gardens and grounds, their landscaping thought to date back to the seventeenth century but which were significantly altered in the nineteenth and twentieth centuries. In 1815 Captain Robert Lisle Coulson, who was born in 1780 and became a captain in the Royal Navy in 1809, had married Sarah Veitch, the heiress of Houndwood. He died in 1822; his widow Sarah and their unmarried daughter Elizabeth Anne then lived together in the mansion for sixty years until Sarah's death in 1882 at the age of 86. Afterwards Elizabeth lived on in the mansion accompanied by a cook, house maid and sewing maid until her own death in 1911 at the age of 92, after which the whole of the household furniture was sold. Since then the property has changed hands several times and in 2015 was advertised for sale for offers in excess of £850,000, subsequently reduced to £780,000.

Hume Castle lies three miles south of Greenlaw off the B6364 road. Although there is evidence of a church being in existence in Hume in 1127, gifted to Kelso Abbey by the Earls of Dunbar, a new church was built in 1147 which lasted until 1560. Hume parish originally belonged to the family of Home but it wasn't until the 1st Earl of Marchmont bought the parish from them in 1766 that the spelling of the name changed from Home to Hume. The first castle here was built in the thirteenth century and, because it stood over 700 feet above sea level, it was used as a beacon station for sending messages to warn the Scots when the English appeared to be about to invade. In 1460 King James II of Scotland and his queen stayed here during the siege of Roxburgh Castle where he was accidentally killed by an exploding cannon. As possession of Home Castle was essential for controlling the East March it was besieged and captured by the English in 1547, 1549 and 1569 but each time was recaptured by the Scots. During the 1547 siege, when Lord Home was lying seriously ill in Edinburgh, the castle was held for Scotland by Lady Home with only a limited number of defenders but the English captured her young son and she surrendered when they threatened to hang him before her eyes. In 1650, when Oliver Cromwell's army under Colonel Fenwick called on the governor, William Wastle, to surrender the castle, Fenwick received the defiant reply that they had never heard of General Cromwell and accompanied it with the message that '*I, Willie Wastle / Stand firm in my castle / And a' the dogs o' your toun / Canna ding Willie Wastle doun*'. Brave words indeed, but the English had brought along six great guns and a mortar piece and after the third volley Willie's nerve failed him and he surrendered the castle. Colonel Fenwick allowed the garrison to leave with their heads high, then demolished the castle in 1651. However, in 1794 the then owner of the estate, the last Earl of Marchmont, built this replica ruin of its outer walls as seen here although the original site was larger than the area he enclosed.

A later story of Hume Castle concerns the events of the evening of 31 January 1804, at the height of Britain's fear of invasion by Napoleonic forces, when a sergeant new to the area was standing sentinel on the ramparts of the castle beside a beacon which he was instructed to light if he saw one begin burning further south at Doolaw. His beacon would, in turn, alert other sentinels to the north and west of Hume to light theirs and so the news would spread throughout the Borders that a French army had invaded and so the militia would be called out. But what the unfortunate sergeant saw was a fire lit by the charcoal burners at Shareswood Colliery. He immediately lit his beacon, other beacons were lit in the Borders upon his signal and by the time the mistake had been realised the militia had hurriedly turned out and assembled in several Border towns. In this more recent picture the houses have been somewhat refurbished compared to their condition in the previous picture and nowadays they have been turned into very attractive residences.

JV 59740

The oldest part of Hutton Castle near Chirnside is the square tower or keep at its south-west corner and this is said to date from around 1200. During the late fifteenth and early sixteenth centuries the castle belonged to the Kers of Samuelstown, but in 1532 the property was purchased by the Homes. In 1544 it was besieged and captured by an English army which then 'burned and spoiled it' but in 1573 Alexander Home began to rebuild and enlarge it into a square tower attached to a long mansion whose patchwork structure originated from various dates. In 1640 the Homes sold the castle to Archibald Johnston, a successful Edinburgh merchant whose family held it for nearly two centuries until it was sold again, firstly to Mr Mackenzie Grieve in 1831 and then by Colonel Robert Johnston to Sir Dudley Coutts Marjoribanks in 1876. By this time much of the original tower had collapsed. Marjoribanks was created Lord Tweedmouth in 1881 and he and his son began repairing, restoring and refurbishing the castle and adding a fourth storey. The son died in 1909 and in 1915 the third Lord Tweedmouth sold the house and its 672-acre estate for £23,000. The household effects were sold over two days at the beginning of April 1916 and bidders came from miles around. Prices were ridiculously low and were generally quoted in guineas (1 guinea = £1.05); typical examples were a 200 guinea billiard table sold for 34 guineas, a Chippendale wardrobe for 36 guineas, a Chippendale mahogany dressing chest fitted with mirror, toilet and morocco-covered writing board and silver handles for 17 guineas, a Sheraton folding card table for 8 guineas, twelve carved oak chairs for 36 guineas, a carved oak sideboard for £11.10s and a mantelpiece clock by LeRoy et Fils with decorated dial on a blue china lyre-shaped stand, decorated with chased ormolu festoons and figures, for £6. The buyer of the estate was Sir William Burrell who decided to house some of his famous collection here and, needing more space for this project, he engaged Sir Robert Lorimer to enlarge the house in 1916; then in 1926 he engaged Reginald Fairlie to carry out further restoration and alterations. However, in 1944 Sir William gave his entire collection to the city of Glasgow, together with £250,000 for the cost of creating a building to house it. This was done and after his death in 1958, in accordance with his will, the interiors of the dining room, hall and drawing room were stripped out of Hutton Castle and reconstructed in his new building in Glasgow's Pollock Park that now houses what has become known as the Burrell Collection. All of this left Hutton Castle in a sorry state and at one time the shell of the house faced demolition but luckily it was saved and refurbished and is nowadays a private house.

This gateway stands at the entrance to the east driveway up to Hutton Castle. The walls are of sandstone but the piers are of pink sandstone ashlar and are crowned with carved stone Berwickshire bears.

Justice Hall which is situated on the northern edge of Oxton was built around 1739 by James Justice who was one of the principal clerks of the Court of Session in Edinburgh. He was a keen horticulturist but this hobby ruined him financially, particularly because he used to buy rare Dutch tulip bulbs that cost as much as £50 each. In 1735 he was forced to sell his estate at Crichton near Edinburgh and four years later he purchased land at Oxton to build this house with the residue of the sale proceeds. After his death the estate was inherited by the son of his second marriage who was born around 1755 and entered the army as an officer in the marine service, attaining the rank of captain. Back at Oxton he showed a great interest in the theatre as well as writing and performing in amateur theatricals but his life then took a turn for the worse. He made an unhappy marriage which ended in separation from his wife and he was pursued by the new proprietors of the Crichton estate in respect of apparently perpetual liabilities that his father had incurred when he sold the estate. Captain Justice challenged the legality of these assertions and the Court of Session ruled in his favour but their decision was reversed by the House of Lords. Faced with these inherited liabilities and heavy legal costs he was forced to sell his Oxton estate in 1816 and move into a cottage in the village where he died in 1823. In 1856 John James Parker obtained a life rent on the land and buildings but the new proprietors lived far away in Cheltenham and took no interest in the property. In 1899, around the time of this photograph, it was recorded by Archibald Allan that 'there was a forlorn look about the house as if it had seen better days and many of the fine trees planted around it by Mr Justice have been cleared away. The fine entrance from the bridge had been rooted out and nothing left of it. The proprietors are all absentees'.

Kames House is situated between Eccles and Birgham and dates from the mid-seventeenth century. The estate belonged to Henry Home who was born in this house in 1696 and became one of the leaders of the Scottish Enlightenment, numbering John Home, David Hume and James Boswell among his friends and associates. An advocate by profession, he was raised to the Bench in 1752 and ennobled as Lord Kames. He was a noted agricultural improver and philosopher and he also made additions to the mansion in the mid-eighteenth century. After his death in 1782 the house was bought by Captain Thomas Riddell who changed its name to Bessborough after an East Indiaman ship he had commanded from 1773 to 1775 but when the estate was purchased in 1825 by the Weir family they reverted to the original name. It descended from them by marriage to the Cosens family, from whom it was purchased in 1912 by Colonel Charles Thomson Menzies who was Joint Managing Director and later Chairman of the publishing house of John Menzies Limited and who immediately employed the architect Harry Ramsay Taylor to reconstruct the mansion. This picture shows the house before Taylor's reconstruction and additions to the right hand side of the building.

Kelloe House, situated about three miles east of Duns and about one and a half miles south of Edrom, was owned by the Buchan family for more than a century before being almost completely demolished in the late 1970s leaving only the former butler's wing, stables and coach house. The 1871 census shows the family to have been living there in some style and it comprised retired colonel George William Fordyce Buchan, aged 59, his wife Anne, aged 40, their son George Charles, aged three, and daughters Laura Elizabeth, seven, and Edith Mary, six.

The domestic staff of Kelloe House comprised a governess, butler, footman, groom, nurse, nursery maid, housekeeper, house maid, under-house maid, kitchen maid and laundry maid. Their cook presumably had a day off. But later that year the *Berwickshire News & General Advertiser* reported the death of the colonel who, as George William Fordyce, had succeeded to the estate in 1856 on the death of his uncle, George Buchan, and had assumed the name of Buchan. In 1858 he had married Anne Dalrymple Ross and they had taken up residence at Kelloe. After his death in 1871 his widow Anne lived on at the house for several more years and the 1891 census shows her to be living with her elder daughter Laura and a slightly reduced staff who now comprised a lady's maid, butler, cook, two house maids, kitchen maid, laundry maid and two grooms.

Kimmerghame House lies about three miles south-east of Duns and was built on the site of an earlier house owned by the Home family. The lands and estates came into the ownership of the Swinton family in 1776 when Archibald Swinton of Manderston married Henrietta Campbell of Blythswood in Glasgow. The Swintons are an ancient family that can trace its roots back to the ninth century and are reported to have been given the name of Swinton for their achievement in clearing the area of wild boar. This creature is prominently displayed in their coat of arms and in the effigies on the gate plinths in the picture. Records show that from the thirteenth to the end of the eighteenth century the family were adept at changing sides to suit the prevailing political climate in spite of a hiccup following King Charles II's restoration to the English throne when Sir John Swinton, the nineteenth of that ilk, was imprisoned for having been one of Oliver Cromwell's most trusted men. However, the family's estates were restored to them following the Glorious Revolution of 1688. In 1825 William Burn had produced designs for a new house but nothing was done about it at the time and the house pictured here was designed in the Scottish Baronial style by the architect David Bryce and built between 1851 and 1853, incorporating some interior panelling from the earlier house. Unfortunately, in 1938 the house was in the process of being updated to add electricity when a workman's error led to a major fire breaking out which destroyed the main part of the building. Fortuitously, nearby Stichill House was being stripped of its fittings and its timbers were used to repair some of the damage at Kimmerghame, principally to the servants' quarters and the main entrance tower. However, when war broke out in 1939 the remaining unrepaired part of the house was demolished and its stone used in the construction of Charterhall Airfield. As a result the whole of the main building to the right of the entrance doorway in the picture is no longer standing.

The lower picture shows the rear of Kimmerghame House before the fire; subsequently the part to the left of the picture was largely demolished. The site of the earlier house (pre-1851) is in the sunken gardens in the foreground. Nineteenth-century census records show that the family was usually absent from the house on the night of the census, probably living in their Edinburgh property, but the 1881 census found them at Kimmerghame and records Archibald Campbell Swinton, aged 68, a landed proprietor and advocate who was not in practice, together with his wife Georgina, aged 57, and his unmarried son John, who was only 23 years old but already a justice of the peace. The family was completed by his daughter Alice, aged 20, and they were served by a cook, lady's maid, late nurse, two house maids, two laundry maids, kitchen maid, footman and a groom. No mention is made of a butler; he may have been absent, living in a separate house or maybe they managed without one. Today the house remains in the possession of the Swinton family, its present owner (2015) being Major General Sir John Swinton who is a former Lord Lieutenant of Berwickshire and father of the Oscar-winning actress Tilda Swinton.

Ladykirk House, situated just north of the River Tweed opposite Norham, was built in 1797 in the Palladian style by the architect William Elliot as a simplified version of Sir William Chambers' Dundas House (nowadays the Royal Bank of Scotland) in St Andrew Square, Edinburgh. In 1845 the architect William Burn made various alterations and additions to the building and the pictures in the house included works by many eminent artists. The estate covered upwards of 150 acres and the proprietor, William Robertson, had a mausoleum for himself built in the grounds but it was never used; when he died in 1830 he was buried within Ladykirk church. The subsequent family history is quite convoluted. William's granddaughter, Marianne-Sarah Haggerston, married David Marjoribanks in 1834 and he changed his name to Robertson. During his lifetime he served as Master of the Berwickshire Hunt, Lord Lieutenant of Berwickshire and Liberal Member of Parliament for Berwickshire. In 1873 he was raised to the peerage as Baron Marjoribanks of Ladykirk but died only seven weeks later after being knocked down by a horse-drawn bus outside his club in Newcastle-upon-Tyne. He had no male children so his title became extinct and after his widow died in 1889 the estate came into the possession of his eldest daughter Sarah who had married Watson Askew of Pallinsburn in 1856. In 1890 he assumed by royal license the name and arms of Robertson of Ladykirk and died in 1906 aged 72, but Sarah lived until her ninety-third year, dying in 1929.

The Robertsons maintained a substantial household at their Ladykirk mansion. The 1851 census shows the occupants to be David Robertson, aged 53, described as a landed proprietor and justice of the peace, his wife Mary, aged 35, and their daughters Sarah, aged 14, and Alicia, aged 9, and son Thomas, aged 7. The family was serviced by a butler, under-butler, footman, under-footman, lady's maid, housekeeper, cook, nurse, nursery maid, three house maids, two laundry maids, two kitchen maids, diary maid and a stillroom maid. That's an indoor staff of eighteen and there would still be the coachmen and grooms living in their own accommodation in the stable block. The 1861 census shows that David was now lord lieutenant of the county but he died in 1873 and the 1881 census shows his widow Mary, aged 65, alone in the house apart from a staff comprising two butlers, footman, hall boy, lady's maid, housekeeper, cook, three house maids, two laundry maids, kitchen maid, scullery maid, diary maid and stillroom maid! The family suffered a tragedy in 1894 just after Mary's granddaughter Bridget, the eldest daughter of Mr and the Hon. Mrs Watson Askew-Robertson, married Captain Raleigh Gilbert Egerton of the Queen's Own Corps of Guides at Norham Church on 22 August. They left for India on 1 October and she died on 23 November almost immediately on arrival. The mansion appears to have been used less and less after Sarah Robertson's death in 1929 and was finally demolished in 1966, being replaced by a modern house built on the site of the old house's formal gardens.

This was the lodge at the north entrance to Ladykirk House and was designed by the Newcastle architect John Dobson (1787–1865) who is perhaps best known for his design of the magnificent Newcastle Central railway station. It was built in the late 1850s in polished pink sandstone ashlar in a single storey, classical-style three-bay cruciform plan with two Tuscan pilasters flanking the four-panelled door. The building initially served as both gate lodge and post office for the nearby village of Upsettlington.

The design of Ladykirk House's West Lodge was inspired by Robert Adam's 1773 entrance screen at Syon House, Middlesex. Ladykirk's spectacular lodge and screen was constructed by William Elliot in 1799 and features columned screen walls, lodge pavilions and a Corinthian archway surmounted by a lion with a rigid outstretched tail which is the emblem of the Percy family. Not surprisingly it was known locally as the Lion Lodge. For over thirty years during the second half of the nineteenth century the gatekeeper living in the lodge on the left of the picture was the widowed Elizabeth Millar and her three unmarried children.

Ladykirk House's stables were designed by George Tattersall in 1845 and the adjoining riding school was completed by H.S. Ridley after Tattersall's death in 1849. The stables are U-shaped in layout and are entered through the arch that is surmounted by a tall octagonal ribbed dome. They are Palladian in style and cost £11,836 to build. Unlike the house, both the stables and riding school still stand.

The Nisbet family owned the Lambden estate at Greenlaw from about the middle of the eighteenth century and in 1839 Robert Nisbet built this classical-style house with its Roman Doric entrance portico off the A697 road. The house was constructed in grey sandstone ashlar with droved ashlar dressings at the front and was extended to the rear in the 1890s to provide more service accommodation. His son James Nisbet, the last male proprietor of the name, died unmarried in 1908, aged 67, and his sisters who succeeded him lived in England so his executors put the estate up for sale in 1916. It was purchased by David Paton Thomson, a member of the Paton family of Alloa who owned the famous yarn spinning business there. He used it as a country retreat but by 1920 the estate had passed to Moffatt Scott Thomson who further extended the service accommodation and refurbished the interior of the house in contemporary 1920s style, much of which still survives. The Thomson family still own the property today.

The ownership of the lands of Langton dates back to the time of King David I of Scotland who granted them to Roger de Ow. The original Langton House or Tower was a little way from the house pictured here and was the home of the Cockburns for many years. In 1758 the estate was purchased by David Gavin, a well-to-do merchant, who built a new mansion house and then felt that the nearby village that he could see from his windows was an eyesore. He had it demolished and the villagers were re-housed about half a mile away in a new village that David named after himself – Gavinton. After this, the line of succession to the estate becomes convoluted. His daughter married John Campbell, the 4th Earl and 1st Marquis of Breadalbane, and it was their elder daughter, Lady Elizabeth Maitland Campbell, who in 1831 married Sir John Pringle, Bart. of Stichill and Newhall and inherited the Langton estate in 1862 on the death of her brother, the 5th Earl and 2nd Marquis of Breadalbane. Shortly before his death the Marquis had begun to rebuild Langton House to the designs of David Bryce into the mansion pictured here, built entirely of ashlar masonry, and by virtue of his bequest the house contained a magnificent gallery of paintings from his principal home at Taymouth Castle, amongst which were some of the best and most valuable works of the leading masters including Anthony van Dyck, Rubens, Velasquez, Raeburn and Landseer, as well as a fine collection of armour. When the building was finished in 1866 Sir John and Lady Elizabeth Pringle moved there from their other home at Stichill but Sir John died in 1869 and Lady Elizabeth lived on in the mansion until her death in 1878, aged 83. The 1871 census shows the mansion's establishment at its greatest, the occupants being Lady Elizabeth Pringle, aged 76, plus her son-in-law Robert Hamilton, aged 42, and her daughter Mary Hamilton, aged 37, together with a housekeeper, two lady's maids, two house maids, two kitchen maids, stillroom maid, laundry maid, diary maid, under-butler, footman, under-footman and a page. There would obviously have been a butler but he was absent on the day of the census. The census also listed Hannah Thorpe, aged 80, described as a Lady and who was living there with her own personal lady's maid.

Things began to go downhill at Langton House after Lady Elizabeth Pringle's death in 1878, partly because the family were hopeless in providing male heirs. After her death the estate passed to her eldest daughter Mary Gavin Pringle who was married to her second cousin, the Hon. Robert Baillie-Hamilton, Member of Parliament for Berwickshire. He died in 1891 and Mary in 1911, after which the estate passed to Mary's younger sister Magdalene Breadalbane Pringle who was by now the widowed Lady Harvey. On her death in 1913 the estate passed to her second son, Major (later Lieutenant Colonel) the Hon. Thomas George Breadalbane Morgan-Grenville DSO MC who assumed the additional name of Gavin on his accession to the estate. By the 1920s the Breadalbanes were in dire financial

straits and in July 1924 they put the entire estate of 1,025 acres up for sale, advertising that the house comprised a hall, picture gallery, four reception rooms, billiard room, boudoir, gun room, ten principal bedrooms and six singles, five dressing rooms, thirteen servants' bedrooms, four bathrooms, nine toilets, five house maids' pantries and ample domestic offices. There were no buyers for the mansion and so in 1925 its contents were put up for sale by auction. Most items sold for less than 25 guineas, typically a carved oak staircase with ten steps being sold for £7 and a shorter one with five steps and a landing sold for £4.5s. No mention was made of the pictures – probably these had been returned to Taymouth Castle. The shell of the house was sold to C. Brand, a contractor from Dundee who was simultaneously demolishing Blackadder House, whilst the *Berwickshire News & Advertiser* of 16 March 1926 reported that 'the walls of the main part of the mansion which were roofless but otherwise intact were sold for 15/- to W. Rodger & Son, builders of Earlston. They also purchased a three-tier fountain that was one of the principal features of the grounds, for £1'. The final indignities were advertisements in local newspapers in 1926 saying that 'its remaining unsold fitments, stonework, stone balusters, coping etc. will be sold cheaply for immediate disposal – apply to the foreman on the job'. In 1931 the building was described as a ruin and it was reported the following year that the parapets on the new Dunglass bridge were being made using stone from the house. It was not until around 1950 that the house was completely demolished and sadly no trace of this magnificent building remains today.

Around 1870 David Bryce designed an impressive Neo-Jacobean gateway for a driveway leading up to Langton House but it wasn't until 1876 that the octogenarian Lady Elizabeth Pringle decided that she wished to beautify the approach to the house by building a straight driveway with Bryce's gateway at the end by the main road. The work was finished at the end of 1876 and had a 100-foot frontage. The principal gate was 12' 6" in width and 22' high including the ornamental top that spanned the distance between the gate piers. They hung from massive ashlar pillars each weighing around 22½ tons that were 4' 10" square and 16' in height, surmounted by scroll finials. The smaller gates on either side were 4' 8" wide and 9' 6" high, finished in stone with their lintels crowned with an elaborate scroll figure. The gates were manufactured by Messrs Sinclair of Leith and cost nearly £500; they weighed around two and a half tons and Lady Elizabeth Pringle's initials in monogram were interwoven in the centre of each leaf on the gate whilst the design above the gate was filled with a figure of the Breadalbane arms. The entire gateway cost more than £3,000. Lady Elizabeth, although in her eighties, took a great interest in the work and paid frequent visits to the workmen engaged on the site; when the project was finished she gave a dinner in the Gavinton old schoolroom to the contractor's 30-odd squad of masons. In order to preserve this gateway and approach exclusively as an entrance for carriages and pedestrians a separate service road and gate lodge were built slightly to the north. These have survived today but both the service road and the main drive lead only to the empty site of the mansion. The great gateway itself, pictured here in 1910, still stands at the side of the A6105 road on the approach to Duns from Greenlaw but the original gates have long gone and in their place are half-height replacements. Another survivor from the past is the Wellingtonia or Giant Redwood tree that was planted by the then prime minister, William Ewart Gladstone, when he visited the house in 1876 and which still stands proudly just inside the gates.

Law House, Coldingham

The mid-nineteenth century Law House at the end of a private road off the A1107 road immediately east of Coldingham village is a good example of a type mass-produced by the well-known architect William Burn. Pictured here in 1903 its frontage has tooled and coursed cream sandstone with sandstone ashlar dressings. Its first owner appears to have been Alexander Thomson Herriot, previously described in the 1851 census as being a farmer of 1,500 acres employing ten men and eight women and living at Northfield but who in the 1861 census is described as being a 64-year-old landed proprietor and Justice of the Peace living at the new Law House. With him were his wife Catherine and unmarried daughter Sarah plus two domestic servants. Alexander died in 1867 and the others were still living in the house in 1871 but Catherine must have died within the next ten years because in the 1881 census 55-year-old Sarah was now living alone in Ayton apart from a single house maid. Coldingham was a favourite area for letting out large houses and villas during the summer to well-off visitors who would bring their entire households including domestic staff with them, staying for several weeks at a time, and this is what appears to have happened to Law House around the turn of the century. The house later changed ownership a number of times, certainly in 1933 and 1947 when it was advertised as having two public rooms, kitchen, back kitchen, pantry, four bedrooms, boxroom, three attics, large bathroom, maid's room and around one and a half acres of land.

The architect of Lees House at Coldstream and its exact date of building are unknown. It certainly existed in the 1770s and shows Adam influences but these may have been added to an earlier building. The estate was the home of a branch of the Marjoribanks family who for centuries were prominent in the affairs of Berwickshire and Edinburgh, providing two Lord Provosts of Edinburgh and Members of Parliament for Berwickshire. The 1871 census shows a very large establishment at the house, comprising Sir John Marjoribanks, aged 40, the 3rd Baronet of Lees, born in 1830 in Madras and landowner and justice of the peace, and his wife Charlotte Athole Mary (nee Trotter), aged 30. Their domestic staff comprised a butler, footman, page boy, lady's maid, housekeeper, house maid, under-house maid, laundry maid, kitchen maid, scullery maid, two grooms and a stable boy. Also living there was Charlotte's unmarried sister, Margaret Catherine Trotter, aged 28, with her own lady's maid. One feature of the family at this time was an inability to produce male heirs and when Sir John died in 1884, aged only 54, the entailed estate passed to his younger brother, Sir William Marjoribanks, who himself died childless only four years later and the baronetcy became extinct.

The year after Sir William's death the contents of his extensive wine cellar were auctioned with cases of Chateaux Margaux 1870 sold for 58/- per dozen, Chateau Latour 1870 for 56/- to 58/- per dozen and Chateau Langos 1874 for 46/- per dozen. Under the terms of the entail the estate was now inherited by his cousin George (later Sir George) Marjoribanks but he regarded the mansion more as a holiday home because he was a partner and later chairman of the world-famous Coutts Bank. The family had a long association with that bank, going back to 1787 when Edward Marjoribanks struck up a friendship with Thomas Coutts who ran a private banking firm. When Sir George died in 1931 the law had changed and the entail was broken so he left the estate to his daughter Monica who promptly sold it. The contents of the house included family portraits and choice pieces of furniture – several by Chippendale – but the highest price realised for an individual item was for an early-eighteenth-century mahogany settee which sold for 130 guineas.

Lees House was sold to Lionel Bird in 1933 but he valued it only for its salmon fishing beat on the Tweed and he let the mansion sink into dereliction. After his death in 1942 his widow sold the house, policies, stables, lodge and fishing rights to the Briggs family for £11,000. Nuns from Newcastle used the house as a summer retreat during and after the Second World War but by the mid-1970s the house was derelict and, having failed to sell it, the owners obtained permission for its demolition. Its destruction was almost completed by the Coldstream fire brigade who burned a good deal of it in 1975 as part of an exercise but it was requested of the demolishers that the two-storey five-bay semi-circular ashlar bow from the garden front should be spared. This was done and in 1980 the architect Nicholas Groves-Raines converted it into a circular house using the Doric portico salvaged from the remains of the frontage. The present owner is Andrew Douglas-Home who made further extensions to the house in 1996 and 1999 and has turned it into his family home.

Sometime around 1820 Thomas Hamilton, 9th Earl of Haddington, commissioned the architect John Paterson to build Lennel House, this two-storey ashlar classical house near Coldstream, on a butterfly plan. Paterson was chief assistant with the Adams' Scottish practice and after their deaths he became the foremost exponent of the Adam castle style. Through marriage with the Baillies the house passed to the earl's descendants, the Baillie-Hamiltons. The 1871 census shows that for whatever reason the house was at that time occupied by Francis Charteris, the 75-year-old Earl of Wemyss & March, Lord Lieutenant of Peeblesshire, together with his wife Louisa and a tremendous domestic staff comprising a valet, lady's maid, chef-de-cuisine, cook, housekeeper, three house maids, kitchen maid, scullery maid, two laundry maids, footman, coachman, under-coachman, groom and under-groom. In the next two censuses the Baillie-Hamiltons were resident and in 1891 the household comprised the retired Royal Navy Commander the Hon. Henry Baillie-Hamilton, aged 58, his wife Harriet Frances, aged 46, and their daughters Helen Georgina, sixteen, Annabel Georgina, fourteen, Katherine Ada Georgina, twelve, Gena Mary, eight, and Margaret Ellinor Georgina, five. Their staff were the German Maria Staner who was described as a teacher plus a nurse, nursery maid, parlour maid, cook, house maid, kitchen maid, laundry maid and stable boy. The Hon. Henry Baillie-Hamilton was the fourth son of George, 10th Earl of Haddington, and died in 1895, aged 63. Beatrix Potter stayed here one summer and it is believed that this is where she had the inspiration for the story of Peter Rabbit which was published in 1902.

In May 1903 the *Berwickshire News* reported that in 'consequence of Lennel Estate, belonging to Lord Haddington, having to be sold shortly, the Hon. Mrs Baillie Hamilton, who has occupied Lennel House for over 30 years, has bought a piece of ground in the village of Newtown'. The estate was purchased by Walter Waring who in 1901, as a wealthy young officer in the 1st Life Guards, had married Lady Clementine Hay, the only daughter of Lord and Lady Tweeddale. Walter had served with distinction in the Boer War and had been awarded the Queen's South Africa Medal with six clasps. During the First World War the house was used as a convalescent home for British, French and Belgian officers suffering from shell-shock which was at that time called a neurasthenic condition. Officers of the rank of major and above were placed under the care of neurology specialists and recuperated there until either being discharged from the army or returned to the front line. They were welcomed at the house by Lady Clementine Waring who in 1918 was awarded the CBE and the medal of Elizabeth of the Belgians in recognition of her work. During this time Major Waring was away fighting in France, Morocco and Salonica and his private study was appropriated as the officers' mess. Amongst the officers who convalesced here was the poet Siegfried Sassoon. After the war the house returned to being a family home and Walter resumed his peace-time profession as Liberal Member of Parliament for Banffshire until the 'Khaki Election' of 1918, after which he served as Coalition Liberal MP for Blaydon until 1922 and then National Liberal MP for Berwick and Haddington until 1923 when he lost the seat. He died in 1930 but the house remained in the family's possession for several more years; it was offered for sale on a number of occasions until finally in 1987 it became the Lennel House Care Centre providing nursing and residential care for older people.

Linthill House, standing off the B6355 road between Ayton and Eyemouth, dates back to the first half of the seventeenth century and is nowadays known as Old Linthill House to distinguish it from the newer farm to the west. Built on an L-plan and three storeys high plus an attic, at some time in the past the main entrance was moved to its present position in the centre of the first floor wall and is accessed by a short flight of stone steps. Following the 1726 marriage of the Rev. Ninian Hume of Billie and Margaret Hume, daughter of Sir George Hume of Wedderburn, they made Linthill their home and after Ninian's death in 1744 Lady Billie personally rode around her estate accompanied by her trusted butler, Norman Ross, to collect the rents from her tenants. These she kept in a strong box under her bed with the keys under her pillow; the door to her bedroom was held fast by a combination lock known only to herself and Ross. One night in 1751 she caught him in the act of trying to steal the keys and, despite having her throat cut, she rang an alarm bell and her killer, trying to escape his fellow servants by leaping from a first floor window, broke his leg. He was captured and taken to Edinburgh for trial, where he was sentenced to be hanged in chains from the Gallowlea between Edinburgh and Leith. His was the last recorded case of the old Scots Criminal Code whereby the offender's right hand was cut off prior to execution. As if Mrs Hume had not suffered enough, her funeral cortege was en route for her last resting place at Bunkle Kirk when it was realised by the inebriated mourners that her coffin had been left behind!

One of Ninian and Margaret's nine children, Patrick, inherited Linthill House but following a Grand Tour in Europe he apparently thought that this was too basic a home so on his return he set about building Paxton House near Berwick-upon-Tweed in 1758 as somewhere more fitting for a European gentleman to live. However, he even lost interest in Paxton when he inherited Wedderburn Castle in 1766 and lived there instead. Today, Linthill is still owned by the Homes of Wedderburn and is rented out as self-catering holiday accommodation.

Longformacus House, situated around six miles north-west of Duns, was built to a classical design by William Adam in 1727 for Sir Robert Sinclair, the 3rd Baronet of Longformacus who died the same year as it was completed. Further additions were made by architect John Smith around 1847 and these turned it into a seven-bay rectangular house. A north wing that was added in 1884 by Robert Rowand Anderson was later demolished. This photograph dates from Edwardian times when the owner was Colonel Alexander Murray Brown. He was the son of the Hon. Forbes Scott Brown who was born in 1816 at Penang, Malaya, and died there in 1874. Alexander was very influential in establishing plantations in that country and in 1868 Queen Victoria appointed him one of the Members of the Legislative Council of the Straits Settlement. He served in the British army and spent a considerable part of his life abroad. In 1869 he married Helen Lydia Kirkpatrick, who was born in 1845 in Kingston, Ontario, and their only daughter, Helen Margaret Brown, was born in 1875. Alexander retired from the army in 1873 with the rank of captain and shortly afterwards was appointed colonel of the Berwickshire Rifle Volunteers, finally retiring with the rank of honorary colonel. He took up residence at Longformacus in 1883 and a few years afterwards succeeded to the estate on the death of his aunt. Alexander died in 1921 and his wife in 1924, but their daughter Helen lived on in the house and this is probably her in the photograph. She inherited the land of Kampung Buah Pala in 1938 and subsequently gave the land to a housing trust under her name for the Tamil workers of her family's firm of Brown & Co., of which she was the last owner. She also took a very active part in local social affairs until her death in 1964.

Maines House near Chirnside was built in 1834 to replace a former house that stood 120 yards to the west and throughout the second half of the nineteenth century it was owned by the Grant-Suttie family. They were descended from George Suttie of Addiston who was created a baronet of Nova Scotia by Queen Anne in 1702 and who married Miss Semple, heiress of the Balgone estates. His grandson, the third baronet, married Agnes, daughter of William Grant of Prestongrange and in due course his son Sir James (the 4th baronet) succeeded to the Prestongrange estate in 1818 and assumed the additional name of Grant. His son was Sir George Grant-Suttie, now titled 5th Baronet of Balgone and Prestongrange, and he married Harriet, daughter of Francis Charteris, the 7th Earl of Wemyss. Their heir was Sir James who was born in 1830 and who left Merton College Oxford with an M.A. degree in 1856; in the following year he married Lady Susan Harriet Innes-Ker, elder daughter of the Duke of Roxburghe. He also joined the Haddington, Berwick, Linlithgow and Peebles Artillery Militia as a junior officer, rising to become its lieutenant-colonel in 1875. But then things began to go wrong for the family because he died in 1878 at the age of 48 and only four months later his successor, Sir James, also died leaving the latter's eight-year-old son George as the 7th baronet. He became a confirmed invalid and lived mainly out of Scotland; a *curator bonis* was appointed to look after his affairs and when he died unmarried in 1947, aged 76, the baronetcy passed to his first cousin once removed and the next heir of entail. By that time Maines House had long since been sold; in the Edwardian period it had been purchased by Edinburgh solicitor Andrew Hogg Glegg and after his death in 1945 it became the home of Colonel and Mrs G.R. Trotter. It is nowadays the luxurious ten-bedroom Chirnside Hall Country House Hotel.

MANDERSTON DUNS.

The first Manderston House was built in the 1790s on a square plan for Mr Dalhousie Weatherstone but in 1855 the estate was bought firstly by Richard Miller and then, on Richard's death in 1864, by his younger brother William Miller. William was both a businessman and a politician. He made a fortune trading hemp and herrings with the Russians and after sixteen years as Honorary Consul at St Petersburg he returned home to become a Liberal MP, firstly for Leith and then for Berwickshire, during which time he was created a baronet in 1874 for political services by Prime Minister William Gladstone. Deciding that the house was too small for his wealth and status, he commissioned the architect James Simpson to add a pillared entrance porch and additional servants' quarters beneath a French Renaissance-style roof. He naturally intended to leave the estate to his eldest son but unfortunately this son died in 1874 by choking on a cherry stone whilst still at Eton so when Sir William himself died in 1887 the baronetcy and Manderston Estate passed to his 24-year-old second son, Sir James Miller, who has been described as a perfect gentleman, a great sportsman, an excellent shot, a horse-racing enthusiast and a gallant soldier. In 1893 he married the Hon. Eveline Curzon, the cultured daughter of the fourth Baron Scarsdale and sister of George Nathaniel Curzon who, as Lord Curzon, subsequently became one of the youngest viceroys of India. Their home at Kedleston Hall in Derbyshire was one of the architect Robert Adam's greatest creations and, not to be outdone, Sir James Miller set out to convert Manderston into a mansion worthy of his bride. He commissioned the Scottish architect John Kinross firstly to build a boathouse in the form of an Alpine chalet and then, in 1895, the stable block and various other buildings. These were meant to be a test of Kinross's ability to build a magnificent mansion and he passed with flying colours. The Boer War temporarily delayed further work but following Sir James's return from active service, work was resumed in 1902 in completely remodelling the house. When Kinross enquired about how much he was allowed to spend on the rebuilding he received every architect's dream answer: 'It simply doesn't matter'.

John Kinross kept the symmetrical Georgian style of Manderston House and created a new north front with an elegant Ionic portico. The family coat of arms was placed above the new main entrance to the house and bears their motto: *Omne Bonum Superne* which translates as 'All good comes from above'. He also built a new bachelors' wing for guests and converted the original stable block into a laundry and staff accommodation and laid out gardens covering 56 acres. The house incorporated the best of Edwardian mod-cons including electricity, plumbing and central heating. Its sumptuous staterooms included a ballroom, marble floors and a wonderful

silver staircase. Domestic staff comforts were not forgotten either; the kitchens in particular were particularly well-designed for their time and staff accommodation was above average standards. When the house was finally completed in November 1905 Sir James and Lady Miller gave a sparkling ball in celebration but very soon the celebrations turned to tragedy when Sir James caught a chill which turned to pneumonia and he died childless on 22 January 1906. The estate now passed to his younger brother John but when he in turn died childless in 1918 it became the property of his eldest sister Amy Elizabeth Miller. In 1866 she had married Major-General Thomas Manbourg Baillie JP and the estate has descended from them through marriage to the present owners who are Lord and Lady Palmer of Huntley & Palmer biscuit fame. The house contains a Biscuit Tin Museum of their products stretching back to 1868.

This is the frontage of the magnificent stables at Manderston House that were built by James Kinross in 1895 in the Georgian style at the same time as the gamekeeper's cottage and kennels and the Buxley Home Farm. The stables cost £20,000 to build and Sir James Miller was so pleased with the result that he commissioned Kinross to go ahead and build his new mansion nearby. Over half a century later the *Berwickshire News* reported in 1948 that their roof of selected teak was arched like that of a church and the stalls were also made of teak with polished brass posts. The names of the horses that once occupied the stalls were on marble panels, the tiled feed troughs were set in teak and all the door fittings and halter rings were of the finest brass. The harness room was a polished masterpiece of rich mahogany with a floor of marble and the harness was massaged on an exquisite table of brass and Italian marble. Sir James's horses won the Derby twice – in 1890 with *Sainfoin* and in 1903 with *Rock Sand*.

It is believed that these ornate iron gates at Manderston were obtained from a house in London on behalf of Sir James Miller by Lord Joseph Duveen, the famous art dealer. He had them gilded, from which they acquired their nickname of the 'Golden Gates'. Lord Duveen was also responsible for acquiring most of the statues in the garden for Sir James. This tripartite gateway has four corniced and channelled pillars which are surmounted by cherubs in various poses.

This picture shows a corner of the Drawing Room at Manderston House. It was one of only three rooms to survive from the earlier Georgian house but in this picture it had been completely redecorated in the Edwardian style of the new house. The walls were cream velvet done with gold and the room displays the cluttered interior typical of the period.

THE MANSE, LAUDER.

This former manse for Lauder church was built in 1812 as a five-bay, two-storey-and-attic house with an attached single-storey service wing and a detached single-storey stable wing. It is a good and little-altered example of a large and prosperous parish manse dating from the time when the well-to-do minister's stipend was £272 per year, and it has fine interior detailing with ornate cornicing, decorative friezes, dado panelling and original fireplaces. The incumbent at the time of the picture was the Rev. Thomas Martin MA who had been inducted as minister in 1876. The 1901 census shows him to be a 55-year-old bachelor looked after by his housekeeper, a 46-year-old widow named Elizabeth Galloway. Thomas was a popular figure in the parish but in 1903 he became unwell and fainted in the pulpit during a sermon. In spite of immediately taking a holiday his health never fully recovered and he died the following year after a brief illness. He was succeeded by the Rev. Walter Lamb BD who unfortunately developed acute pneumonia after attending a meeting of the General Assembly of the Church of Scotland and died in 1906 after only fifteen months in the post. A few weeks later the Rev. William McConachie BD was inducted and he ministered at Lauder until his death in 1931.

At one time the Marchmont estate was the largest in Berwickshire and stretched from the Tweed to the Lammermuirs. It also included land in Lauderdale and belonged to the Earl of Marchmont and his successors, the Hume Campbells. The grounds, covering around 390 acres, began to be laid out before the house was built, commencing in 1726 with the planting of a Great Avenue with 10,000 Dutch elms. This avenue is one and a half miles long and is thought to be the longest in Scotland. Marchmont House was built in the Palladian style by Thomas Gibson (who is believed to have been working to William Adam's designs) in 1750 for Hugh Hume, the third Earl of Marchmont, and alterations were subsequently made to the rear elevation by the architect William Burn between 1834 and 1842. The last of the family, Sir John Hume Campbell, sold the house to the advocate Robert Finnie McEwen in 1913 and the house appeared at that time as shown in the first picture dated 1903 (left, bottom). However, between 1914 and 1917 McEwen commissioned Sir Robert Lorimer to add a top floor with dormer windows in a steeper pitched roof and to connect the flanking pavilions to the house as seen in the later 1923 picture of the rear of the house (below). The ground at the front of the house was lowered and a new main entrance was created in a porch; the former entrance became the central window of the first floor saloon and can nowadays be seen above the main entrance. The interior of the house was not neglected either. Mr McEwen had inherited a considerable fortune and put it to good use, including the transposition of the library and the dining room and the creation of a grand double-storey music room out of the stable wing in the north pavilion. On the outbreak of war in September 1939 the staff and pupils of John Watson's School in Edinburgh were evacuated to the house for a time. Following the death of Sir James McEwen in 1983 the house was sold to Sue Ryder Care Homes who opened it as a care centre for young sick and disabled people in 1989. Unfortunately it proved too expensive for them to maintain and had to close in 2007 but the house was subsequently acquired by the present owners of the Marchmont Estate who are restoring it to its former glory.

The principal Mellerstain lands had belonged to the de Haitley family since the twelfth century but over the succeeding four and a half centuries the properties changed hands numerous times among the notable Border families. In 1642 they were made over by royal charter to George Baillie of Jerviswood, the son of a prosperous merchant burgess of Edinburgh, and he lived in a tower house on the site of the present house near Gordon. When he died in 1646 he was succeeded by his eldest surviving son, Robert, but in 1684 Robert was arrested and executed because of his opposition to the government of the Catholic King James II. His son George managed to flee to Holland but the family estates were confiscated; however they were restored when George returned with the victorious Protestant William of Orange in 1688. In 1725 he began building Mellerstain House, about eight miles north of Kelso, to the design of William Adam, the father of the more famous Adam brothers, but only the two wings of this Palladian-style house were ever built. For some forty years the East wing was used as the family's residence and the West was used for servants' quarters and stables. In 1759 George Baillie's grandson, also called George, inherited the estate. He was the second son of the Earl of Haddington; he changed his surname to Baillie and in 1770 he commissioned Robert Adam to design a new house to join up the two wings. Adam, working to a relatively tight budget, designed the house in a 'castle' style which was cheaper than a 'classical' style (rough chiselled stone as against expensive dressed stone) and it was completed in 1778 as seen in this picture of its north front.

This picture shows the south front of Robert Adam's design of Mellerstain House. It subsequently passed through marriage to the Hamilton family of Haddington and in 1858 the house was inherited by George Baillie who became the 10th Earl of Haddington and added Hamilton to his name. When the family inherited the Arden estates they also added that name to their surname for a time! The family owned a number of estates in England and Scotland, notably Tyninghame in East Lothian and Arden in Cheshire and both the Haddingtons and their eldest son, Lord Binning and his family, appear to have divided their time between them. In November 1897 the *Edinburgh Evening News* reported that since the summer of 1842 the house had not been occupied for long periods so that it had got into a state of utter disrepair but at present it was undergoing extensive renovation with the view of Lord and Lady Binning taking up residence early the next year. One consequence of these renovations was that the workmen making alterations broke through a wall into a previously unknown cellar that was well-stocked with liquor, some of the bottles bearing the date 1825. In 1870 Sir George Baillie Hamilton Arden succeeded to the earldom as the 11th Earl of Haddington and died, aged 89, in 1917, having never got over the shock a few weeks earlier of the death of his 61-year-old son and heir, Brigadier-General Lord Binning (the Hon. George Baillie Hamilton). The earldom devolved on the latter's 21-year-old eldest son who, it being wartime, held a commission in the Scots Greys. The present owner of Mellerstain is the 13th Earl, John Baillie Hamilton, and the house remains one of the finest stately homes of Scotland.

THE LAKE, MELLERSTAIN, GORDON

Robert Adam was also commissioned to landscape Mellerstain's surrounding area, including the creation of a lake. He did this in the style of a Dutch Canal, surrounded by raised grass walks on which classical statues were placed at intervals. Nothing remains of this today because in 1910 the lake was altered and enlarged by Sir Reginald Blomfield, who created this Italianate formal terraced garden linked to the house with steps that lead down to wide lawns and give views of the Cheviot Hills in the distance.

The beautifully proportioned library at Mellerstain House is one of Robert Adam's most impressive interiors. The delicate plasterwork includes large Wedgewood-esque plaques portraying classical themes, and the ceiling is regarded as one of his masterpieces. The decoration includes paintings and sculptures of classical figures such as Minerva, Priam, Achilles, Iphigenia and Hercules, as well as portraits of contemporary figures such as Lady Grizell Baillie, wife of George Baillie and their daughter, Lady Murray. The chimneypiece is of white marble with black marble backgrounds to the fluting and patera ornament.

This picture shows the gates at the West Lodge entrance to the Mellerstain estate with the long drive up to the house, known as the 'Long Straight', disappearing into the distance. These gates are flanked by two more similar gateposts situated at each end of the railings, with the lodge itself just out of sight on the right of the picture.

Mersington House, about four miles from Greenlaw, was built around 1865. The house stands next to a field containing the turf-covered footings of a range of buildings that indicate that it was once the site of a medieval village. Historical documents show that a tower and chapel (the latter first recorded in 1250) stood at Mersington until 1545 when the Earl of Hertford destroyed both in a raid. The chapel was subsequently rebuilt but no trace remains of it today. The Mersington estate comprised the house, farm and around 561 acres of land including a number of houses in Leitholm and the Leitholm Grass Parks. Its first owner appears to have been Lieutenant-Colonel Nesbit, an eminent agriculturist and a breeder of pure shorthorn cattle and Leicestershire sheep who died in 1865. He left the estate to his son, also Major Nisbet, but he died five years later in 1870, aged only 40. In 1875 the whole estate was sold for £50,000 to Thomas Scott, a farmer of 2,300 acres at Morebattle where he employed six men, twelve women and two boys. He and his family moved into Mersington House which in due course was inherited by his son John Scott.

In 1905 41-year-old John Scott of Mersington House married 39-year-old Isabella Gentle of Collessie, Fife. She became a keen follower of the Berwickshire Hunt and was an expert golfer and a good shot with a shotgun. The picture on the previous page shows the couple with their two dogs in the grounds of their house in 1907. John died in 1923, aged 59, but Isabella outlived him by fourteen years, dying in 1937 at the age of 71. There were no children of their marriage and the estate was sold that same year to William Logan of Kinleith near Edinburgh.

Mertoun (Merton) House stands on the River Tweed two miles north-east of St Boswells. The estate was originally a property of the Halliburton family and they built a two-storey harled and crowstepped house in 1677 but around 1680 they sold their estate to Sir William Scott of Harden. In 1703 his grandson commissioned Sir William Bruce to build a new mansion on the estate and the result was the three-storey pedimented house that forms the central part of this picture. Sir Walter Scott, a relative of the family, was a frequent visitor and he wrote his poem 'The Eve of St John' here in 1799. In 1843 the architect William Burn added a south wing to the house but this wasn't balanced until 1913–16 when architects Gibson & Gordon added a north wing. The picture shows the house in this form, the two taller wings rather overwhelming Bruce's original building. The 1891 census shows a large establishment to match; it comprised Walter Hugh Hepburne Scott (Lord Polwarth), aged 52, his wife Mary, aged 46, two sons, five daughters, a governess, butler, lady's maid, housekeeper, three house maids, kitchen maid, dairy maid, two laundry maids, scullery maid and two footmen. In 1912 the Scotts decided to return to their original home at Harden, south of Hawick, and the Mertoun estate, totalling 6,550 acres, was purchased for £256,000 by John Egerton, Viscount Brackley, who later became the 4th Earl of Ellesmere. In 1956 he engaged the architect Ian Gordon Lindsay to remove the two wings, thus reducing size of the building to Bruce's original house. In 1963 John Egerton's son, the 5th Earl of Ellesmere, became the 6th Duke of Sutherland and Mertoun House is nowadays that family's home for a good part of the year. The 26-acre gardens are open to the public but the house is private. The original house of 1677 still stands within the walled garden and is now the head gardener's residence.

This picture is included because of its dramatic view of Milldown House and Milldown Burn which flows down this rocky gorge to join the sea at Coldingham Bay, just to the south of St Abbs. Until recently the burn could only be crossed by means of stepping stones but a footbridge has now been erected in the foreground of the picture, a feature much welcomed by walkers because there is usually considerably more water in the burn than in this picture.

The origins of Milne Graden have an interesting history. In 1816 a British fleet sailed to Algiers in an attempt to suppress the piracy of the North African Barbary States, who were enslaving European Christians, and in particular to persuade the Dey of Algiers to forgo this practice. Negotiations failed and so the British fleet bombarded the port of Algiers and destroyed its navy. The second-in-command of the British fleet was Rear Admiral David Milne aboard HMS *Impregnable* and out of the spoils of victory he was able to purchase the Milne Graden estate a few miles north-east of Coldstream in 1821. The following year he commissioned James Gillespie Graham to build this neoclassical mansion on a site overlooking the Tweed. The north elevation has pediments and a portico but the south elevation was built with twin bow fronts to capitalise on the view. Dormer windows were added by John Lessels in 1852–53.

Admiral Milne died in 1845 and was succeeded in the Milne Graden estate by his son David who achieved success as an advocate, landowner, geologist and meteorologist. He was President of the Edinburgh Geological Society from 1874 to 1889 and was elected a Fellow of the Royal Society of Edinburgh as early as 1828 when he was only 23 years old. In 1832 David married Jean Forman Home of Paxton, Berwickshire, but after succeeding to the Milne Graden estate in 1845 he gave up legal practice and lived the life of a country gentleman, improving his and his wife's estates and devoting as much time as possible to scientific pursuits. In 1852 his wife inherited her father's estates at Wedderburn, Billie and Paxton and they took the name of Milne-Home.

In 1872 one of their five daughters (Margaret) married naval officer Charles Hotham and the 1881 census records a household comprising David Milne-Home, aged 76, a widower described as a landed proprietor and magistrate; his son-in-law Charles F. Hotham, aged 39, a post-captain in the Royal Navy, and his wife Margaret, aged 43, together with their three young children Jean, John and Alan. There were also David's four unmarried daughters, Jean (47), Grace (45), Georgina (34) and Susan (29). The domestic staff that day comprised two lady's maids, a nurse, nursery maid, butler, two footmen, housekeeper, three house maids, two laundry maids, kitchen maid, scullery maid, diary maid and a groom. The cook must have had a day off. After David's death in 1890 at the age of 85, the Hothams inherited the estate and the 1901 census finds their family living in Admiralty House, Portsmouth, where Charles was designated Admiral of the Fleet Sir Charles Frederick Hotham. Milne Graden was left in the care of Thomas Renton who had previously appeared in the 1861 census as the family's young page boy.

Nenthorn House stands off the A6089 road near the left bank of the River Eden, four and a half miles north-west of Kelso. This three-storey mansion was built after 1862 as a replacement for Old Nenthorn House and has been attributed to the Edinburgh architect Thomas Leadbetter who designed it in what has been called a 'Jacobethan' style, using features characteristic of Elizabethan and Jacobean architecture. It was the home of Frederick Lewis Roy JP who was born in 1836, succeeded to his estates of 1,826 acres in Berwickshire and Roxburghshire in 1868, and died in 1906. A few years earlier he had sold the property to Mr and Mrs George Ritchie who lived there until 1911 when it was purchased from them by Mr and Mrs Martin Joseph Fernandez Ferreira. In 1919 the proprietors became the Thomson family who lived there for many years but in 1990 permission was given for the house to be converted into a 40-bed Nursing Home. This was not a financial success and in 2003 a change of use from a nursing home to a dwelling house was authorised. However, by 2006 the house was in a sorry state and it was not possible to enter the building because of concerns over its structural integrity but since then it has been restored and extended.

Nenthorn House from the weir on the River Eden that held back the fish pond. The building on the right contained the sluice for the pond.

Nenthorn Old House stands to the south-west of its successor and is thought to date from the early eighteenth century. It fell out of regular use after the present Nenthorn House was built but was sometimes used for events such as parties for local children, schools and estate workers. It fell into total disuse during the early twentieth century and became a roofless shell with no trace remaining of the crow-stepped gable above the main entrance. Happily, in recent years the shell of the house was purchased privately and the new owners have rebuilt it into an attractive-looking though smaller house.

The Netherbyres at Eyemouth was owned for at least 250 years by the Craw family, one of whom built the harbour at Eyemouth, but in 1827 it was purchased by Captain Sir Samuel Brown RN (1776–1852) who engaged the architect George Angus to build this house in 1834–35. Constructed with great rolling Victorian bargeboards, it was enlarged in the 1860s and later in the 1930s. This picture dates from 1906.

Captain Sir Samuel Brown was a celebrated engineer of his time. When he retired from the Royal Navy in 1812, after patenting a type of anchor chain that was still in use a century later, he went on to design and patent chain suspension piers and bridges including in 1820 the Union Chain Suspension Bridge over the River Tweed between Horncliffe in Northumberland and Fishwick in Berwickshire. At the time of its construction it was the longest wrought-iron suspension bridge in the world with a span of 449 feet and is the oldest suspension bridge still carrying road traffic because it narrowly pre-dates Thomas Telford's suspension bridge over the Menai Straits. Costing £7,700 to build, it has been strengthened and refurbished on a number of occasions. In 1823 he built the Chain Pier at Brighton, immortalised in John Constable's famous 1827 painting, and also made the chains for the launch of SS *Great Eastern* that are pictured in the famous photograph of Brunel standing beside them at the launch site at Millwall. Captain Brown died in 1852 having sold the estate only eight days previously to William Mitchell-Innes of Ayton Castle. In 1861 William passed it to his son, Alexander Mitchell-Innes, who promptly assigned it to John Ramsay L'Amy who had married his sister. In 1880 L'Amy sold the properties to Alexander Gibson, a director of the Royal Bank of Scotland, who gave them to his son William in 1898. Eventually the house was bought by Sir Christopher Furness in 1928 and his second son, Colonel Simon Furness, subsequently donated it in the 1980s to the Royal Gardeners' Benevolent Society for charitable use. In 2007, as part of a cost-cutting exercise, the society transferred ownership to the Leonard Cheshire Foundation but they in turn were forced to close the home in 2013 as it was no longer economically viable as a retirement home.

The former lodge at the gates to Netherbyres House. Now only the truncated gate piers remain.

The Newton family held the lands of Little Newton near Kelso until 1648 when they sold them to Alexander Don. He retitled himself as the first Don of Newton Don and was created the 1st Baronet in 1667. The 6th Baronet of this line was Sir Alexander Don who was born in 1779 and succeeded to the estate in 1815. He commissioned Sir Robert Smirke to rebuild Newton Don House in 1817–20 as this three-storey neoclassical adaptation of an earlier building overlooking the Eden Water for which Robert Adam had prepared plans in the eighteenth century but the expense crippled Alexander financially and he had to sell off parts of the estate. He died when his son, Sir William, was only eleven months old and by 1846 most of the estate had been sold. The remainder was sold in 1847 to Charles Balfour of Balgonie in Fife and that family still owns the estate to this day, meaning that since the fourteenth century the estate has been owned by only three families: the Newtons, the Dons and the Balfours. A notable resident for much of the twentieth century was Major Charles James Balfour DL of the Scots Guards, who was born in 1889 and married in 1917 the Hon. Aurea Versa Baring, daughter of Francis Edward Denzil Baring, 5th Lord Ashburton and a member of the famous Baring banking dynasty. Charles died in 1939 but Aurea survived until 1975. During both the First and Second world wars the house was turned into the Newton Don Auxiliary Hospital for wounded soldiers and evacuees from Edinburgh also came to live here during the Second World War; among them for a short period was the comedian Ronnie Corbett.

70

Ninewells House near Chirnside derived its name from the springs that flow from the hillside into the Whiteadder Water. The original house on this site was the childhood home of David Hume (1711–76), the Scottish Enlightenment philosopher who changed his surname from Home to Hume because the English insisted on pronouncing his name incorrectly. This house was replaced by the one pictured here which was designed in the Tudor style by William Burn in 1839–41 for Elizabeth Hume. That family subsequently married with the Ross family and adopted the name of Ross-Hume. James Alexander Ross-Hume succeeded to the estate in 1864 at the age of twelve and lived until 1935. During the Second World War the house was used as a hostel for displaced Polish and Eastern European personnel; some Polish army personnel were also billeted here as well as in Chirnside village and around 1942–43 it was in use as a prisoner-of-war camp. The house never recovered from this treatment; it was roofless and derelict by the early 1960s and was completely demolished in 1964.

Nisbet House lies about three miles south of Duns and was built in 1630 by Sir Alexander Nisbet soon after his marriage to Katherine Swinton. Unfortunately for him, he and his five sons supported the Royalist cause in the English Civil War: his eldest son Philip took part in Montrose's Highland campaign and was present at the Battle of Philiphaugh, from which he escaped but was later captured and executed. Philip's younger brother Robert joined Montrose's last expedition to Scotland but they lost at Invercharron and he was taken to Edinburgh and executed, whilst a third son, Major Alexander Nisbet, was killed at the siege of York in 1644. Sir Alexander himself was reduced to poverty and had to sell the estate to John Ker of Cavers in 1652. Ker's descendants added an impressive tower, probably designed

by William Adam, to the west end of the house in 1774. A description of the house in 1915 said that the kitchen, servants' hall and ancillary rooms were on the ground floor whilst the first floor contained the drawing room, dining room and library, the latter two rooms made out of the original 40-foot-long Great Hall. The second floor had four bedrooms and three bathrooms whilst the third floor had three bedrooms and a bathroom. The estate remained in the possession of the Ker family (latterly in the person of Lord Sinclair) until the 1950s when they sold the estate to Lord Brocket. He partly modernised the house and in turn sold it to a local farmer in the mid-1960s. Subsequently the house was unoccupied for several years but it was later resold and has now been comprehensively restored into an impressive private house.

Northfield House, which is situated off Coldingham Road at St Abbs and on the cliffs known as 'Black Craighead' just north-west of the village, was completed in 1892 for Andrew Usher who owned a large whisky distilling business in Edinburgh and had purchased the Northfield estate in 1885. He was a noted philanthropist who funded the building of the Usher Hall in Edinburgh, whilst in St Abbs he funded the building of the local school in 1887, the church in 1892 and the building of the outer harbour in 1890. He also changed the name of the village from Coldingham Shore to St Abbs. In 1897 his eldest daughter, Jane Binning Usher, married the artist and explorer William Gordon Burn-Murdoch and when her father died the following year she was left the life-rent of Northfield estate. They didn't occupy the house the whole time; it was frequently let to tenants and in 1921 its contents were sold by auction. Typical prices paid were a Chippendale 2-leaf mahogany inlaid table sold for £7.10s, a Chippendale semi-circular table for £8.15s, twelve dining room chairs in Morocco leather for £36 and a large carved oak sideboard with mirror, drawers and cupboards for £39. Following Jane's death in 1927 the house was advertised for sale at an asking price of £7,000 which included seven acres of garden, garage, stables, chauffeur's, gardener's and keeper's houses, kennels, electric generating plant, grazing and arable lands, the Mire trout loch and various feus and leases at St Abbs Head. The house was still being advertised in 1928 so there can't have been any acceptable offers in 1927. Eventually the house was purchased by Lord Amulree who used it occasionally as a summer residence, letting it out to tenants at other times. He was said to be a brilliant lawyer who had unusual gifts as an arbitrator and the government of the day used his skills on a number of occasions. In 1930, at the age of 70, he succeeded the deceased Lord Thomson as Secretary of State for Air in Ramsay Macdonald's government until the general election held the following year. He died in 1942 and in 1948 his successor to the property advertised the whole estate for sale. The house was described as having four sitting rooms, six principal bedroom and dressing rooms, two bathrooms and servants' quarters. Many years later, in 2006, the house itself was sold for £1.3 million. The greenhouse/veranda sheltering the entrance tower has now gone and so has the decorative ironwork on the top of the tower but otherwise the house looks the same as in the picture. The building on the left is its ballroom.

Oxendean Tower, which stood in countryside a little over a mile north-west of Duns, was described in 1862 as 'a commodious dwelling house two storeys high, with offices, garden and small ornamental garden attached'. Plans of the estate from 1786 show it to have been the property of James Auchenleck of Oxendean but it appears to have been leased out to various tenants during the nineteenth and twentieth centuries. One of these tenants was John Brooks who lived there with his wife and son in the summer months from the 1880s until 1901, wintering in Algiers where he had an estate. In 1901 he took a lease of a mansion at St Germains near Longniddry and it was there in the following year, shortly after returning from Algiers, that he began acting strangely and three weeks later shot dead both his wife and himself in their bedroom with his sporting rifle. Meanwhile Oxendean Towers was let to Major (later Lieutenant-Colonel) J.W. Currie of the Indian Staff Corps but ultimately, like so many other mansions, it was too expensive to maintain in post-war years and was demolished in the 1960s.

Although this aspect of Paxton House, six miles from Berwick-upon-Tweed, overlooks its formal garden its appearance is less impressive from this side than on the opposite side which has a colonnaded entrance and is flanked by two large wings. The house was built of pink sandstone in the Palladian style for Patrick Home of Billie between 1858 and 1863 and is believed to have been designed by the brothers John and James Adam. However, before the house was completed Patrick inherited the family seat of Wedderburn Castle; he moved into the castle and lost interest in his great new house which he then sold in 1773 to his cousin Ninian Home. Ninian and his wife Penelope commissioned the third Adam brother, Robert, to carry our further interior decoration and Thomas Chippendale to furnish the house. Ninian owned two sugar plantations on the island of Grenada and in 1793 he was appointed its governor. The couple returned to the island but unfortunately Penelope died very shortly afterwards and Ninian was killed in 1795 when the French invaded the island. As the couple were childless Paxton House was inherited by Ninian's brother George Home, an Edinburgh lawyer. As well as the house George also inherited a very large collection of books, paintings and objects d'art that Patrick had collected many years earlier whilst on the Grand Tour with the intention of displaying them at Wedderburn. The large drawing room there proved too small to display the collection which was then left unopened in packing cases. George wished to display these treasures at Paxton House so he commissioned the Edinburgh architect Robert Reid to design a large extension which became known as the Regency Wing; it was completed in 1814 and was furnished by the famous Edinburgh firm of William Trotter.

After George's death the house passed to his cousin who adopted the family name to become John Foreman Home, then through a succession of Milne Homes and finally to the present-day Home-Robertsons. The three central bays on the ground floor in the picture contained the housekeeper's room, her storeroom and a pantry with the dining room above them on the first floor. To the right of the dining room was the drawing room and to its left and on the second floor were bedrooms. A small portion of the Regency Wing can be seen on the right of the picture. Nineteenth-century censuses show that the family was rarely in residence, the house usually being let to well-off tenants, but the census taken in 1881 is particularly interesting because the parents (Lieutenant-Colonel and Mrs David Milne Home) were away and their children left behind in the house were their eldest son David W. Milne Home, aged seven, with two younger sons aged six and four, plus two daughters aged two and seven months. The list of the staff shows that the Downton Abbey television programmes did not exaggerate the pecking order amongst domestic staff: present at the census were a head nurse, second nurse, third nurse, cook, housekeeper, second house maid, head laundry maid, under-laundry maid, diary maid, scullery maid, groom and general servant.

Peelwalls is an early-nineteenth-century mansion that stands off the B6365 road about a mile south-west of Ayton village. The original mansion house here stood in the present kitchen garden and the new house was built nearby in the Classical style with a five-bay front and a Doric pilastered doorway using stone from the Cullaloe Quarry in Fife. It was accessed by a sweeping driveway. In the lower picture the modern B6365 road runs past the gates from the left and disappears to the right with the mansion house visible in the background. In the middle of the nineteenth century the house was owned by the Dickson family and subsequently, through marriage, by the Cosens. Next came John Mickle and his family and when a later owner, retired farmer and landowner John Allan died in 1910 at the age of 88, the house comprised a hall, dining room, drawing room, parlour, library, bedrooms, pantries, kitchen, milk house and wash house. A subsequent owner was John Darling Smith, a county councillor and justice of the peace, who died in 1955. Eventually the house was bought by Intensacare Ltd who converted it into the Borders Nursing Home which housed 26 residents and had plans to build a small village for elderly persons in the 30-acre site with the mansion at its core, providing all necessary services to the village. Unfortunately the plans for the village did not materialise after only five houses had been built; they were never occupied and the nursing home itself closed in 2008. There are currently plans to build a further 26 houses on the site and to convert the mansion, which has 20 bedrooms and eleven bathrooms, back to residential use.

Two identical lodges were built around 1830 at the north and south entrances to the driveway up to Peelwalls House. These pictures show the South Lodge that still stands by the pillared entrance to the driveway up to the mansion; judging from the man's clothes he is very likely the estate gardener. The lodge is nowadays screened from the B6365 road by trees but the pillared gateway and gates still stand as in the picture although the left hand pillar is now obscured by a growth of creeper.

Standing by the Ale Water two miles west of Coldingham and four miles from St Abbs, Press Castle is an early nineteenth century battlemented house with Gothic features but its origins date back to the early 1600s. During the nineteenth century it was the country home of two Lord Provosts of Edinburgh but in 1889 the estate was purchased by George Denholm, an Edinburgh stockbroker who shortly afterwards also became Consul for the Argentine Republic and Mexico. While quite a young man he had been appointed confidential secretary to David Robertson of Ladykirk, afterwards Lord Marjoribanks and MP for Berwickshire, and the 1871 census finds him living at Mr Robertson's house in Upper Brook Street, London, with thirteen staff including three footmen, two lady's maids and two butlers! George Denholm was an avid collector of autographed items, particularly letters written by famous people, as well as a wide range of curios. One of these was the ornamental brass knocker on his front door which had been placed on the barrier at the Edinburgh city boundary when King George the Fourth visited the city in 1822. The king had to alight from his carriage and knock for admission to the city before being formally received and welcomed by the magistrates. George Denholm died in 1905 leaving the immense (for those days) personal estate of almost £20,000; his widow lived on in the house for a number of years but in 1917 the estate was sold to John Story Vaux, a member of the Durham brewing family. Unfortunately he ran into financial problems and in 1921 he attempted to sell the estate; no-one would buy the mansion house but its contents were sold over two days. It can be gleaned from the sale particulars that the house comprised an entrance hall, drawing room, dining room, billiard room, breakfast room, business room, nine bedrooms, housekeeper's room and butler's bedroom. Things went from bad to worse for Mr Vaux; he was declared bankrupt in 1926 and died suddenly the following year. In the meantime the estate was purchased for £12,500 by George Davidson, a farmer of Mountfair, Swinton, and comprised the mansion house, lodge, garage, stables, gardens, and Press Mains farm, all amounting to 662 acres. Also included was a bathing chalet at nearby Coldingham Sands that was rented out during the summer months. Mr Davidson didn't enjoy his new estate for long: he died in 1929 and was succeeded by John Davidson who died as recently as 2013. His agricultural contracting firm of J.N. & W.S. Davidson operated from the house for many years but nowadays it is divided into a number of individual apartments.

The history of the Purves estate dates back to 1624 when King James VI devised the Baronetage of Nova Scotia as a means of financing the plantation of that province by creating 100 baronets, each of whom had to support six colonists for two years or pay 2,000 marks in lieu. In addition they each had to pay 1,000 marks to Sir William Alexander to whom James had granted the colony by charter in 1621. In 1685 Sir William Purves was created a Baronet of Nova Scotia and the 1st Baronet of Purves Hall. Over the years the family added other surnames to their own; the eighth and last baronet being Sir John Home-Purves-Hume-Campbell who

died in 1960, whereupon the title became extinct. The original Purves Hall was a pele tower situated to the north of the present hall and an account in 1858 describes it as being 'an old mansion house about four storeys high and almost in ruins'. The present building, pictured here in 1903, was built in the later part of the nineteenth century as its replacement. This classically-styled two storey house is built of sandstone masonry with a slated roof and has a seventeenth century window incorporated into its south-west wall that probably came from the older building because it has a carved panel bearing the date 1675. A large walled garden that was built in the late eighteenth or early nineteenth century and was originally attached to the older house is situated immediately to the north of the present-day house.

Rathburne House in Longformacus, six miles north of Duns and pictured here in 1908, was built in 1898–1900 as a shooting lodge for the well-travelled civil engineer and Indophile Charles Henry Holme. He was an avid hunter and the various rooms in the house displayed the trophies he had collected over many years. At the time they were regarded as one of the finest private collections of this kind in the United Kingdom but most visitors to the house nowadays would have been appalled. The items on display included the skins and heads of Indian crocodiles and tigers, the hides of leopards, stags, a Himalayan black bear and a sloth bear plus stag and antelope horns and the head of an Indian buffalo. A photograph on the wall proudly displayed his 'bag' of seven tigers and five leopards on a 40-day shooting trip in India. A lesser diversion occurred in 1907 when his chauffeur was fined for having driven a car recklessly in the streets of Kelso, causing the horses of a carriage to swerve. He was fined £5 with the option of ten days imprisonment! The hall/lounge was the centrepiece of the ground floor accommodation with a magnificent plastered ceiling and an elegant broad staircase leading to the mezzanine and first floors.

Mr Holme died in 1928 and two years later the estate was offered for sale with the mansion described as comprising on the ground floor the hall/lounge, drawing room, dining room, library and smoking room whilst the upper floor had eight bedrooms, two dressing rooms and bathrooms. There was also ample servants' and kitchen accommodation plus outside offices, garage, stables, three houses for estate servants, electricity and gravitational water supply. The whole estate, comprising around 23 acres, was offered for sale for £3,000 and appears to have been purchased by the 8th Duke of Roxburghe and tenanted by Lieutenant-Colonel Wilfrid Richardson Peacock Henry, late of the Indian Army 12th Cavalry. However, in 1948 the house was sold to Mr and Mrs Gore Graham and in August they opened the house as the Rathburne Hotel but could not obtain a bar licence from the Berwickshire Licensing Court because of strong objections received from the Kirk Session of Longformacus and the Temperance Committee of Duns Presbytery, and also from the Chief Constable of Berwickshire who said there would be difficulty in the police supervising the hotel which lies out in the countryside. In the meantime the new owners installed running water in the guest bedrooms and provided two toilets to serve the nine bedrooms. Mrs Helen Graham was the hotel's licensee and eventually obtained a bar license in March 1951 at the seventh attempt in spite of continued objections from the kirk and the chief constable who thought it was unnecessary to grant a license even though there was not another licensed premises within eight miles. A seven-day license was granted by a majority decision of the court. In its time as a hotel it featured a small golf course and mini railway in its grounds, artist studios, a library, music rooms and an exhibition space that housed an annual show of Scottish paintings. In 2002 the hotel was purchased by the Norley family who restored the house and also the grounds which had been damaged when the previous owners had used them for the commercial rearing of wild boar and stags. They ran the house as a bed and breakfast establishment but for family reasons they put the house up for sale in 2008 when it achieved a selling price of £965,000.

Renton House is a classical three-storey mansion situated close to the village of Grantshouse and overlooks both the old and the new A1 roads. It was built in the early eighteenth century of whinstone with dressed sandstone margins and with the later addition of the two-storey pedimented stepped portico. The Barony of Renton is an ancient one and is first mentioned in the early twelfth century. The male line died out in 1498 and down the years the barony passed through marriage to the Elloms, the Homes and finally, in 1783, to the Stirlings of Glorat. They sometimes let out the house to tenants and at one time it was used as an upmarket inn before the Stirlings themselves eventually moved into the house in the 1930s. It has changed hands a number of times since then and is nowadays owned by the Heywood family.

A rear view of Renton House. In 1783 Sir James Home was succeeded by Sir John Stirling, then by Sir John's son, Sir Samuel of Glorat, and then in 1858 by the latter's nephew, Sir Samuel Home Stirling. He died only three years later, aged 31, leaving a young widow and two daughters. Twenty years later the census shows the household in 1881 to have been Mary (the Dowager Lady Stirling), aged 51, and her daughters Mary Eleanor Stirling, aged 25, and Edith Home Stirling, aged 21. The domestic staff comprised the housekeeper, house maid, sewing maid, laundry maid, kitchen maid, coachman and groom. Mary Eleanor was the heiress to the estate and in 1885 she married Charles Lisle Cookson who added his name to hers. Mary died in 1898 and the 1901 census shows the household at that time to be Charles Lisle Stirling-Cookson, aged 46, and his children Mary Eleanor Olive, aged eleven, Samuel, aged nine, and Marguerite, aged two, supported by a governess, nursery maid, cook, table maid, house maid, kitchen maid and laundry maid.

Retreat House, a late-eighteenth-century two-storey circular building which is harled and designed with Gothic windows and a conical slated roof topped with central chimney stack, stands near the A1 road at Grantshouse. In 1806 the *Gazetteer of Scotland* reported that 'The Earl of Wemyss has lately built an elegant sporting villa called the retreat about a mile from the small kirkton of Abbay' (i.e. Abbey St Bathans).

Rhymers Tower is named after Thomas Learmont (*c*.1220–*c*.1297), also known as Thomas of Ercildoune (Earlston) or Thomas the Rhymer. He was a local landowner, poet and seer whose youth was reputedly marked by a seven-year spell in Fairyland after he fell asleep one day under the Eildon Tree and kissed the Queen of the Fairies. Returning eventually from Fairyland older and much wiser he became famous for his predictions over the next seven years before he is said to have vanished for good, presumably back to Fairyland. The first printed book of his collected prophecies was published in 1603. One of these was his accurate prediction in 1286 of the accidental death of King Alexander III. The ruins of this small whinstone pele with walls four feet thick stand off the A68 road at the approach to Earlston village from the south but whilst they are known as the Rhymers Tower they date from the sixteenth century, three centuries later than Thomas's time. In these two pictures the walls are completely covered in ivy but nowadays the creeper has been removed and the remains can be properly seen.

Rowchester House is situated about two miles south-east of Greenlaw and was originally built around 1830 for John Castell Hopkins as a castellated Gothic design in cream-coloured sandstone. In 1852 the estate was purchased from Mr Hopkins by Robert Henry Broughton who maintained good relations with his tenants and employees but didn't mix in society or take any interest in public matters. He lived there until his death in 1894, aged 65, when the estate passed jointly to his two nephews James and Frank Marjoribanks. Frank died in 1905 and James made it his home, having the house extended in 1914 by the architectural practice of J.M. Dick Peddie and Forbes Smith who added a third storey in Jacobean style plus garden terraces. After James's death in 1930 the estate was put up for sale in 1935 and comprised the house and four farms plus 20 acres of gardens and 74 acres of grass parks. The house contained three grand reception rooms, thirteen bedrooms and six bathrooms as well as various other rooms; the whole estate was offered for £21,770 or the house itself plus 94 acres for £6,000. The house remained unoccupied until 1939 when it was bought by Lieutenant-Colonel Julius Francis Chenevix-Trench of the Royal Northumberland Fusiliers. He died in 1948 and in more recent years the house was sold in October 2006 for £2.15 million. A popular music festival featuring mainly young bands is held in the park over two days in summer with profits from ticket sales going to charity.

Rowieston Lodge was once located at a T-junction where the A697 main road two and a half miles east of Greenlaw met a minor road leading to Marchmont, but it now stands back a few yards from both thoroughfares due to road improvements having been made over the years. What was once the junction has been bypassed by the main road on a sweeping bend and the lodge, once known colloquially as Inkbottle Lodge because of its shape, is now partly hidden behind bushes. For many years in the nineteenth century it was home to a series of hedgers and their families whilst the 1901 census shows the occupants to have been David Gillies, a gamekeeper aged 35, together with his wife and their six children whose ages ranged from ten years to a baby of a few months old.

Spottiswoode House lay off the road between Lauder and Westruther and was the seat of the Spottiswoodes, a prominent Borders family. There were Spottiswoodes in the area in the thirteenth century and their lands eventually descended to John Spottiswoode, the Archbishop of St Andrews who crowned King Charles I and became Lord High Chancellor of Scotland. He sold the estate to the Bells in 1620 but it was repurchased in 1700 by his great-grandson John Spottiswoode, a distinguished advocate. It is probable that a tower house existed on the site in late medieval times but no trace now remains of it because the family built a new house in the early eighteenth century. In 1832 this house was extended by the architect William Burn who built a new wing to the south-west and altered the original building to match the character of his new addition. The rebuilt house had a very ornate appearance, with curved Dutch gables, dome-topped turrets and elaborate balustrades.

Its best known occupant was probably Alicia Anne Spottiswoode, the elder daughter of John Spottiswoode and Helen Wauchope. Born in June 1809, in 1836 she married Lord John Douglas Montague Scott, a brother of the 4th Duke of Buccleuch but Lord John died in 1860 and Alicia, now titled Lady John Scott, succeeded to the estate on the death of her mother in 1870. In 1835 she had written a tune for a song but when she later read the words of 'Annie Laurie' she decided that they fitted her tune better. Not content with that, she largely rewrote the second verse and added an entirely new third verse, resulting in the song that is so popular today. Even in her old age she lived in the mansion in great style. The 1891 census found her to be 80 years old and attended by a domestic staff of sixteen comprised of a lady's maid, butler, cook, housekeeper, two house maids, two laundry maids, kitchen maid, scullery maid, dairy maid, still room maid, footman, two grooms and a hall boy. She died in March 1900 shortly before her ninetieth birthday and was succeeded by her eighteen-year-old great-nephew, John Roderick Charles Herbert Spottiswoode. By 1935 the estate, which had once covered 9,000 acres, had been reduced by sales of land to only 2,442 acres and that year Mr Spottiswoode ordered a three-day sale of the mansion's contents. The house was said to comprise entrance halls, six reception rooms and seventeen bedrooms and in November 1935 it was offered for sale, together with 107 acres, at a public roup but failed to reach its reserve price of £3,500. Various structural faults had developed over the years; it was eventually purchased in 1937 for its fittings and stonework and was completely demolished in 1939.

At the entrance to the Spottiswoode estate two Gothic arches, each with two tiers of pinnacles and with plaques on their flanking piers, were built spanning the minor road that leaves the A697 road at Dod Mill to the south-west of the house. The first to be encountered is the Pyatshaw Archway (above and right) which today still looks in as good condition as in the picture except that the lettering on the plaque, a poem by Lady John Scott, is weathered and almost illegible. Further along the road, standing by the gate lodge at the end of the driveway up to the mansion, is the Bruntaburn Mill Archway (below) which is nowadays so overgrown with creeper it is almost unrecognisable as a structure.

Spottiswoode Entrance Arch, Lauder

This identical pair of rectangular-plan lodge houses at Spottiswoode were built in 1796 but have since received various additions and alterations. They stand on the A697 road at what was the formal entrance to the driveway up to the mansion. Lady John Scott's motto was 'Haud fast to the past' and she loved reminiscing about the days of stagecoaches. She had the distances to many parts of Britain painted onto the walls of the lodges, those on the East Lodge (on the right of the picture) showing the distances to Morpeth, Newcastle, York, London, Portsmouth and Plymouth whilst those on the West Lodge (below) showed the distances to Crieff, Perth, Aberdeen, Inverness, Dalkeith, Edinburgh, Falkirk and Glasgow. Their two false clocks were painted with the times of 11.11 a.m. and 1.53 p.m. which were the times when the daily stagecoaches were due to pass by. The lodges were sometimes known as the 'Eagle Lodges' because of the stone birds adorning the inner piers of the gates but sadly neither the eagles nor the piers nor the gates themselves are there today.

Overlooking the Tweed at Birgham on the A698 road four miles west of Coldstream, Springhill House was built in the late eighteenth century as the dower house for The Hirsel and therefore was the property of the Earls of Home. Alterations were carried out by the architect William Leitch in 1816 and around 1903 a T-plan wing was built onto the rear in a similar style to the original house. Although a dower house was usually built as a residence for a widow who had to move out of the family mansion when her husband died so that the successor to the estate and his family could move into the mansion, Springhill House was used as the residence of the Earl of Home's

eldest son who had the courtesy title of Lord Dunglass. When an Earl of Home died his son moved into The Hirsel and his own eldest son took over Springhill and the title of Lord Dunglass. Probably the best-known person to hold that title was Alexander Frederick Douglas-Home (1903–1995) who became the 14th Earl of Home in 1951 and renounced his title in 1963; then as Sir Alec Douglas-Home he served as Prime Minister in 1963–64. He retired from politics in 1974 and, because he could not regain his former earldom, he was created a life peer as Baron Home of the Hirsel of Coldstream. This picture dates from around 1906; in the 1980s the house possessed a hall, four reception rooms, eight bedrooms, a shower room and three bathrooms.

This house, situated at the end of a short private road off the B6461 road west of Leitholm, has been variously called Stainrigg, Stanerig, Stanerigg and Stoneridge. The original house, built in 1631, was a three-storey harled structure built along simple classical lines but in 1880 the architectural firm of Kinnear and Peddie carried out extensive work which gave the house a very different, Scots Baronial, appearance. It is not known how much of the old fabric survived internally but no trace remains externally. This rebuilding was commissioned by General John Cockburn-Hood who had entered the Indian Army Staff Corps in 1840 and served through the Punjab campaign of 1848–49 and the 'Indian Mutiny' of 1857–58 before retiring here to his family home. At the time of the 1901 census he was in ill health and is recorded as being a 77-year-old retired army general and a widower. Also living in the house were his unmarried sister Isabella Cockburn-Hood, aged 74, and his great-niece Marion Cockburn-Hood, aged 23 and also unmarried. The household was complemented by a sick nurse, cook, house maid, under maid and table maid. John Cockburn-Hood died only four weeks after the census was taken and was succeeded by John Shapland Elliot Cockburn-Hood who had been born in 1844 in New South Wales, Australia, but had come to Britain and since 1875 had been the vicar of Kirkby Fleetham in Yorkshire. Unfortunately he died following a bicycle accident at Catterick in August 1902. In 1912, around the time of this picture, the furniture in the house was sold and the advertisement in the *Berwickshire News* stated that the house had a hall, dining room, drawing room, library, kitchen and an unspecified number of bedrooms. In 1996 approval was granted to change the designation of the house from residential to conference facilities/residential but in 2002 it was changed back again to residential.

STONESHIEL, BERWICKSHIRE.

Situated on a minor road off the B6437 road south-east of Auchencrow near Reston, Stoneshiel Hall is a two-storey ashlar house of 1840 with hood-mouldings and battlemented skyline. The 1861 census shows the owner to have been Henry Robert Hardie, aged 36, unmarried and a landed proprietor. He died in 1871, his furniture was sold and the house was taken over by a Mr Mickle who was described in the 1881 census as being aged 66, a married landowner and farmer of 190 acres employing five men and six girls. He lived with his wife and daughter, together with a cook, house maid and laundress. Mr Mickle died in 1885 and the house then appears to have been rented to tenants for several years because it wasn't until 1907 that his trustees advertised a sale of his furnishings. The advertisement stated that the house comprised an entrance, inner hall, retiring room, drawing room, dining room, business room, stair and landings, seven bedrooms and dressing rooms, butler's and other pantries, kitchen, scullery and laundry. A two-bedroom cottage named Dovecot Cottage, which was converted from a former lectern-shaped dovecot, is located in a corner of the walled garden. Further owners were a Mrs Collie and then a Mrs Broun, the latter dying in 1945 when her household furniture was sold and both properties, together with 3,413 acres, were bought for £3,250 by Miss Clementina Mary Gordon, a Liberal activist and former active supporter of women's suffrage. In 2014 the two houses and 2.2 acres of grounds were advertised for sale for £650,000, the interior of the hall being said to comprise a reception hall, drawing room, sitting room, dining room, kitchen, five bedrooms and three bathrooms. The large reception hall leads to the drawing room and the sweeping suspended staircase to the first floor whilst the house's original features include solid timber panel doors, servants' bells, working shutters, decorative plaster work and open fireplaces.

Swinton House.

For around nine centuries the Swinton family owned the estate that bears their name and Swinton House, six miles from Duns and Coldstream, was at its core. Around 1060 the family were awarded the whole of the parish by Malcolm Canmore in gratitude for having assisted him to regain his ancestral throne. For a while the land was given to Coldingham Abbey but was restored to the family by a charter granted by King David I, Malcolm's youngest son, who became king after his death. In the seventeenth century the family made the political mistake of supporting Oliver Cromwell and at the Restoration in 1660 their lands were forfeited to the Duke of Lauderdale. However, in another change of fortune the family supported William of Orange's claim to the throne and regained their estates at the time of the Glorious Revolution of 1688. Unfortunately, their years in exile had left them short of money and they were forced to sell some of their property. The original Swinton House on this site was burnt down around 1797 and was replaced in 1800 by this Neo-Classical mansion built by John Swinton who was an advocate and High Sheriff of Berwickshire from 1793 until his death in 1820.

John Swinton, his eldest son, survived his father by nine years and died unmarried in 1829, when the estate was sold to his cousin, Samuel Swinton. It eventually devolved on his eldest daughter Anne Elizabeth who in 1871 had married her cousin George Swinton, Chief Secretary to the Governor-General of India. She became Mrs Swinton of Swinton in her own right and when she died in 1883 her will instructed that the estate should be sold and the proceeds divided amongst the four surviving members of her family. In 1890 the estate was purchased by a Miss McNab at a cost of £52,000 and then purchased from her two years later by her cousin, John McNab, for £55,000. He died in 1902 and his widow immediately sold off his pedigree Clydesdale horses, cattle, sheep and carriages, followed the next year by most of the house's furnishings. She was now the proprietrix; she resided in Edinburgh and leased the house to Mr Thomas Greenshield Leadbetter who occupied it for eight years. After he ended his tenancy Mrs McNab decided to sell the estate for £50,000 and in 1912 it was bought by Captain George Herbert Taylor Swinton, the eldest son of Adam Swinton and grandson of Mrs Anne Swinton. Thus the Swintons came back into their own after the estate had been in other hands for 22 years.

A north block was added to Swinton House in the mid-nineteenth century. As the main entrance is on this part of the house and is offset, it looks as though it may have been a later addition. The house was tenanted by Thomas Greenshields Leadbetter at the time of this 1907 photograph. When the *Berwickshire News* advertised the estate for sale in August 1912 it comprised 1,155 acres including the village of Swinton and two lodges. The mansion house itself possessed an entrance hall, dining room, drawing room, morning room, billiard room, cloakroom, parlour, butler's pantry, day and night nurseries, kitchens, eight bedrooms, two dressing rooms and servants' accommodation.

In 1745 the Temple Hall estate at Coldingham belonged to Sir John Home of Renton but he sold it in 1747 and it passed through no fewer than ten more owners before being purchased in 1894 by Edinburgh-born Robert Fitzroy Bell. He was the grandson of the founder of Bell's Whisky in Perth and in 1884 he had founded the Edinburgh University Students' Representative Council (SRC) which gained statutory recognition in the Universities (Scotland) Act, 1889. He trained as an advocate and when he purchased the estate he commissioned the Edinburgh architect James Jerdan to build this house which was not ready for occupation until 1897.

Robert Fitzroy Bell died in 1908 and the history of Temple Hall over the next few years is unclear but its entire contents were sold by auction in February 1926. In September 1939 various deaf, dumb and blind people were evacuated here from Edinburgh at the outbreak of the Second World War and in 1944 the Quaker-run Barns Hostel School 'therapeutic community' for difficult and disturbed young men was relocated here from their previous home at Barns House near Peebles and was renamed simply 'Barns School'. Unfortunately a major fire broke out in February 1946 which necessitated the school being temporarily housed in Broomlee Camp before moving to Ancrum House; Temple Hall was badly damaged by the fire and was later demolished.

TEMPLE HALL COLDINGHAM, BERWICKSHIRE.

Thirlestane Castle from N., Lauder

Thirlestane Castle lies just outside the burgh of Lauder and is the home of the Earls of Lauderdale who are the Hereditary Saltire Banner Bearers of Scotland and Chiefs of the Clan Maitland. In 1223 Sir Richard de Matulent (or Mautalent) acquired the lands through his wife Avicia, the daughter and heiress of Thomas de Thirlestane, and in 1345 his grandson Robert obtained a charter from King David II of the lands of Lethington (now called Lennoxlove) in East Lothian. From him descended Sir Richard Maitland (1496–1586), judge, statesman, diplomat, antiquary and poet who was very well regarded throughout Scotland, a rarity in those days for someone in public life. His eldest son William (1528–1573) is better known to history as the brilliant but extremely devious Secretary Lethington. As Mary, Queen of Scots' Secretary of State he was generally devoted to her interests but was said to have been involved successively in the murders of both her private secretary Rizzio and her husband Darnley. He lost his position when Mary fled to England and, falling foul of the Regent Morton, was imprisoned in Leith prison where he died. His younger brother John (1545-1595) was a more cautious man who eventually became Secretary of State and was raised to the peerage as Lord Thirlestane in 1590. He decided to build a new castle for himself on the present site to replace the old pele tower.

Thirlestane Castle was transformed between 1670 and 1677 by John's grandson John Maitland, Duke of Lauderdale (1616–1682), who was one of King Charles II's closest advisors. He was a member of the king's famous five-man cabinet council known from their initials as the CABAL (Clifford, Arlington, Buckingham, Ashley and Lauderdale) and the acronym has remained into modern times to denote a clique. Lauderdale employed Sir William Bruce, King Charles's master mason, in conjunction with Robert Mylne; they retained the old castle of 1590 as the central part of the new castle and introduced the two front towers and the grand staircase as well as the transformation of the interior, particularly the ornate plasterwork of the State Rooms. The building was altered again by William Burn and David Bryce in 1840; they added the two outer wings with towers flanking the central keep which has given the castle its present distinctive skyline. But by the time that Captain Gerald Maitland-Carew inherited the castle in 1972 it had been allowed to fall into disrepair with the central tower in imminent danger of collapse and no fewer than forty major outbreaks of dry rot. To save the building from becoming a ruin he gifted it to a charitable trust which, with the aid of financial grants from the Historic Buildings Council and the National Heritage Memorial Fund, has enabled it to be restored to its present excellent condition. This old picture shows the castle viewed from the south-east.

The Maitland coat of arms bears the Latin motto *consilio et animis* ('by wisdom and courage') and is supported by two eagles. These great birds are represented on the gate pillars of the Eagle Gates which guard the entrance to the driveway up to the house off the B6362 road. The rusticated piers and wrought iron gates are still *in situ* today at the main public entrance to the castle.

A charming view of one of the other lodges guarding the driveways up to Thirlestane Castle.

The Maitland family had acquired land at Thirlestane in Lauderdale around 1250 through marriage. An early castle already existed on this site above the Boondreigh Water south of the A697 road but it was either replaced by or incorporated into the later fifteenth century Thirlestane Tower which is pictured here. This had a vaulted ground floor and was originally at least three storeys high, L-shaped and around 33 feet long, 24 feet wide and with walls over three feet thick. This picture shows the south side of the main block, nowadays only 25 feet high, and part of a wing. The tower appears to have continued in use after the Maitlands built their new castle in 1595 but as early as 1771 it was shown on Armstrong's map of the County of Berwick as being in ruins.

This house, once known as 'The Villa' but nowadays named Allanbrae, was built by John Lessels in 1854 at the north-west end of Allanton village overlooking the confluence of the Whiteadder and Blackadder waters. The village formed part of the Blackadder Estate and the villa was a school for the daughters of senior staff on the Blackadder estate. It was rebuilt in 1924 following a fire but closed in 1932 and is now a private house that looks somewhat different to the picture but is still recognisable.

Warden House at Coldingham was built by Edinburgh-based architect James Jerdan in 1902 as a country home for his wife and himself. He was born at Greenlees Farm near Yetholm in 1839, was apprenticed as a joiner and in 1868, by now a twenty-nine-year-old journeyman joiner, he married nineteen-year-old Helen Watson who was a Melrose-born power loom weaver. Around 1875 James joined the Edinburgh architectural practice of Wardrop and Reid but left around 1885 to set up his own practice in Edinburgh. Most of his work was executed in Edinburgh, the Lothians and the Borders. He and Helen raised nine children at their home in Edinburgh, the eldest son John eventually taking over the practice around 1902 when James began suffering from diabetes. He and Helen then retired to Warden House where Helen died in 1909; James died in Edinburgh in November 1913.

The original Wedderburn Castle on this site was a simple tower but it was demolished to make space for a new castle; this was built around the empty space which became its courtyard. The new castle was designed and constructed by the famous Adam brothers (Robert and James) for Patrick Home of Billie, the 13th Baron of Wedderburn, between 1771 and 1775. Its three storeys topped by battlements are typical of the Adam brothers' 'Castle' style and the arms of Wedderburn appear above the porte-cochere which was added in 1820. Whilst the house was being built Patrick Home, like many noblemen of the time, embarked upon a Grand Tour of the continent and sent back many works of art including outstanding chimney pieces which form part of the castle's attractions today.

The lands of Wedderburn are thought to take their name from a clan of the same name, the first person of that name to be recorded being Walter de Wedderburn in 1296. In the fifteenth century the feudal superiority of the lands of Wedderburn belonged to the Earls of Douglas who granted a feu to the Homes in 1413 but by 1550 the Homes themselves had acquired the superiority, a position they still hold today as owners of the estate. The family had a tragic history in the fifteenth and sixteenth centuries: between 1413 and 1576 every first-born son died either in battle or in English captivity. Two of the family died at the Battle of Flodden in 1513, along with their king and hundreds of other Scottish nobles. This picture shows happier times outside the house in the late nineteenth or early twentieth century.

The Lion Lodge, Wedderburn Castle.

Wedderburn Castle is approached from the north through this splendid gate where a recumbent lion sits on top of the arch to guard the driveway up to the castle. The gate was built in 1794 and the boundary walls on either side were built by French prisoners of war captured in the Napoleonic Wars.

In 1258 Wedderlie, four miles west of Greenlaw, was owned by Sir Robert de Polwarth but in 1327 Sir Richard Edgar was granted this property (and more besides in Nithsdale, Dumfriesshire) on account of his backing Robert the Bruce's claim to the Scottish throne. Sir Richard was a witness at Bruce's second marriage and the Edgar family retained ownership of the Wedderlie estate for over 400 years. It was ravaged by English raiders time and time again but in the more peaceful time of 1680 the family built this mansion onto an earlier late sixteenth century tower house. Sir James Edgar, born in 1688, was private secretary to James Francis Edward Stuart (the father of Bonnie Prince Charlie and known as the 'Old Pretender') and was the chief conspirator and mastermind behind the Jacobite rebellions of 1715 and 1745. Unfortunately the family fell on hard times and had to sell Wedderlie in 1733, defacing their family crest on the mansion as they left for good. The purchaser was Robert Stuart, 7th Lord Blantyre, and the estate remained in his family's possession until the beginning of the twentieth century. They don't appear to have cared for the building very well because in 1842 the *Topographical, Statistical and Historical Gazetteer of Scotland* wrote that 'Wedderlie, once a seat but now a mere shooting box belonging to Lord Blantyre, stands at the base of the uplands, and is an ancient structure crumbling into disrepair'. Fortunately by 1884 it had been restored and this picture shows it in 1914 when it was almost hidden behind an immense growth of creeper. During the Blantyres' ownership the house was occupied by a succession of tenants and their families, one of whom was John Clay who was involved in the foundation of the Chicago Stock Yards. In July 1942 the estate of around 3,200 acres was sold to Captain and Mrs Thomas Elliot and has descended through their family to the present day, the house nowadays standing without its creeper.

Standing little more than a mile south of Chirnside, Whitehall House was a large mansion of which only a two-storey portion remains, complete with Palladian windows and rustic porch. The earliest parts appear to date from the early eighteenth century when it was owned by the Hall of Dunglass family. It passed in 1837 to the Mitchell-Innes family of Ayton Castle who extensively remodelled it throughout the 1800s; the first floor music room in particular was richly decorated in Italian plasterwork. Alexander Mitchell-Innes inherited both Ayton Castle and Whitehall in 1860 and the following year's census shows a huge establishment at the house. His first wife, Charlotte Dick-Lauder, died in childbirth in 1848 having their sixth child and in 1852 he married Fanny Augusta Vine and went on to have a further nine children. The 1861 census shows Alexander Mitchell-Innes, aged 49, and described as a landed proprietor, together with his wife Fanny Augusta, aged 39, and a family of five sons and three daughters, their ages ranging from nineteen to a new baby. They were supported by a total of no less than 24 domestic staff who comprised a butler, two footmen, hall boy, two governesses, lady's maid, upper nurse, two nursery maids, wet nurse, cook, housekeeper, three housemaids, four laundresses, kitchen maid, two scullery maids and a still room maid! Alexander died in 1886 and Fanny in 1902 but the family held the house until the 1980s. Since then the house and estate have passed through the hands of developers. The partial demolition of the back quarters of the house left Whitehall completely open and a danger to the public and since 2007 the mansion has been derelict and in a dangerous condition. In 2015 it was advertised for sale for offers in excess of £1 on condition that any bidder could prove that they had the means to restore the property to a wind and watertight condition so that it was removed from the Buildings at Risk Register. The estimated cost of restoration was put at £1.2 million, but there were no buyers so the owners were given permission to demolish the house, which they did in July 2015.

Whitehill House was built in the early twentieth century as the home of Mr George Herbert Jardine Dove, the factor for the Earl of Haddington whose seat – Mellerstain House – is about two miles away. In 2012 the house was extensively refurbished and offered for letting at a rate of £1,700 per calendar month, subsequently reduced in 2015 to £1,600 per calendar month.